TRAMS WEST BROMWICH

INCLUDING SMETHWICK, OLDBURY, WEDNESBURY, DUDLEY AND THE MIDLAND METRO

DAVID HARVEY

AMBERLEY

First published 2015

Amberley Publishing
The Hill, Stroud
Gloucestershire, GL5 4EP

www.amberley-books.com

British Library Cataloguing in Publication Data.
A catalogue record for this book is available from the British Library.

ISBN 978 1 4456 4157 7 (print)
ISBN 978 1 4456 4171 3 (ebook)

Typeset in 10pt on 12pt Sabon.
Typesetting and Origination by Amberley Publishing.
Printed in the UK.

Contents

Introduction

This book is a new prequel to the *West Bromwich Buses* volume and shows the development of tram services in West Bromwich and nearby Smethwick, Oldbury and Dudley from 1883 until 1939. It also includes the Midland Metro system in the West Bromwich area.

Acknowledgements

The author is grateful to the many known and unknown photographers acknowledged in the text whose photographs appear in this volume, all of which were taken over seventy years ago. Where the photographer is not known, the photographs are credited to my own collection.

The two volumes of Stanley Webb's *Tramways of the Black Country* proved a most useful source of information and I am indebted to Roger Smith for producing the three excellent tramway route maps. Special thanks are due to my wife Diana for her splendid proofreading.

The book would not have been possible without the continued encouragement given by Louis Archard and Campbell McCutcheon of Amberley Publishing.

Tramcar Operation in the West Bromwich Area (Including Smethwick, Oldbury, Wednesbury and Dudley)

The tramways in the West Bromwich area, to the west of Birmingham, can be best described by imagining a piece of paper in the landscape format. There is a straight line across at the top, representing the tramlines through West Bromwich, with Birmingham, Handsworth and The Hawthorns to the right and Carters Green, Dudley and Wednesbury to the left. In the middle of this line is West Bromwich town centre, where the tram routes using Spon Lane and Bromford Lane go in a vaguely southerly direction. At the bottom of the page is another line, roughly parallel for most of its length to the first line. This goes again from Birmingham to Dudley, but this time by way of Smethwick. After skirting around the south of West Bromwich at Spon Lane, it carries on to Oldbury, passing Bromford Lane in the middle of Oldbury's Market Place and then onto Brades Village, Tividale. This line then joins the other line from West Bromwich at Burnt Tree before going on to Dudley. Connecting these two lines are two chords using Spon Lane and Bromford Lane mentioned above (see Map 1).

West Bromwich Corporation never operated their own trams, yet running through the town and the nearby towns of Smethwick, Oldbury and Tividale for over fifty-seven years were horse-drawn, steam and electric trams. The track was owned by these local authorities, but leased to operating companies and eventually Birmingham Corporation Tramways Department.

The advantage for the tram operators, especially in the electric tramcar era, was that they all operated on the 3-foot 6-inch gauge, which did allow a certain amount of movement over each other's tracks in order to reach a depot, the overhaul works at Tividale, or to transfer tramcars from one of the Birmingham & Midland Tramways Joint Committee companies to another. This is why the tramcar fleet numbering of the four different companies is often at best difficult to follow, impossible to fathom or impenetrably obscure as records have long since disappeared. The late Stanley Webb's two-part book on the Black Country tramways has been a most valuable source of information but it has taken this writer forty years to actually follow the text, such are the complexities of company tramcar operation in the Black Country!

It becomes easier to understand the routes after 1 April 1924 and 1 April 1928, when in each case company operation ceased and Birmingham Corporation took over the operation of the tramways from the South Staffordshire Tramways (Lessee) Co. Ltd, through

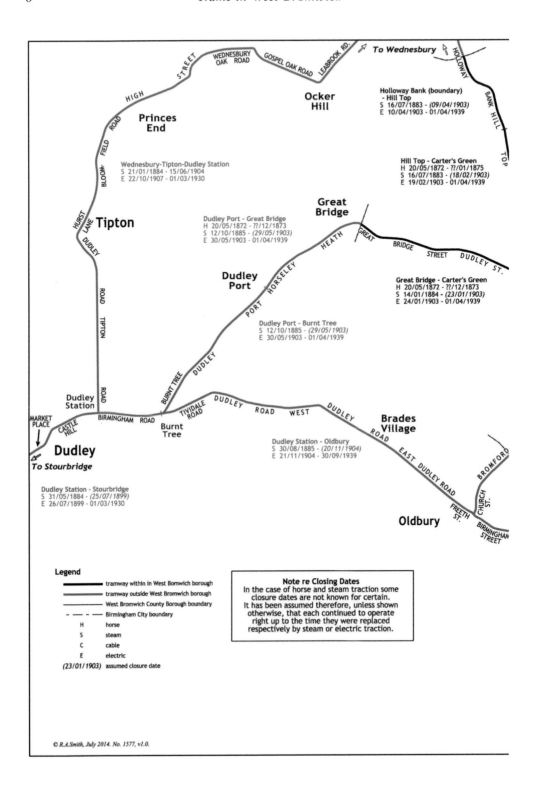

To Wednesbury

WEDNESBURY OAK ROAD   GOSPEL OAK ROAD   LEABROOK RD.   HOLLOWAY

STREET

HIGH

Ocker Hill

Holloway Bank (boundary) - Hill Top
S 16/07/1883 - (09/04/1903)
E 10/04/1903 - 01/04/1939

BANK HILL TOP

Princes End

ROAD

FIELD

BLOOM-

Wednesbury-Tipton-Dudley Station
S 21/01/1884 - 15/06/1904
E 22/10/1907 - 01/03/1930

Hill Top - Carter's Green
H 20/05/1872 - ??/01/1875
S 16/07/1883 - (18/02/1903)
E 19/02/1903 - 01/04/1939

HURST LANE

Tipton

DUDLEY

Great Bridge

Dudley Port - Great Bridge
H 20/05/1872 - ??/12/1873
S 12/10/1885 - (29/05/1903)
E 30/05/1903 - 01/04/1939

HEATH   GREAT

BRIDGE STREET DUDLEY ST.

Dudley Port

PORT HORSELEY

ROAD TIPTON

Dudley Port - Burnt Tree
S 12/10/1885 - (29/05/1903)
E 30/05/1903 - 01/04/1939

Great Bridge - Carter's Green
H 20/05/1872 - ??/12/1873
S 14/01/1884 - (23/01/1903)
E 24/01/1903 - 01/04/1939

BURNT TREE   DUDLEY

ROAD

Dudley Station

MARKET PLACE

CASTLE HILL

BIRMINGHAM ROAD

TIVIDALE ROAD

DUDLEY ROAD WEST

DUDLEY

Brades Village

ROAD EAST DUDLEY ROAD

Burnt Tree

Dudley Station - Oldbury
S 30/08/1885 - (20/11/1904)
E 21/11/1904 - 30/09/1939

Dudley

To Stourbridge

Dudley Station - Stourbridge
S 31/05/1884 - (25/07/1899)
E 26/07/1899 - 01/03/1930

BROMFORD

CHURCH ST.

FREETH ST.

BIRMINGHAM STREET

Oldbury

Legend

▬▬▬▬▬	tramway within in West Bromwich borough
▬▬▬▬▬	tramway outside West Bromwich borough
─────	West Bromwich County Borough boundary
– · – · –	Birmingham City boundary
H	horse
S	steam
C	cable
E	electric
(23/01/1903)	assumed closure date

Note re Closing Dates
In the case of horse and steam traction some closure dates are not known for certain.
It has been assumed therefore, unless shown otherwise, that each continued to operate right up to the time they were replaced respectively by steam or electric traction.

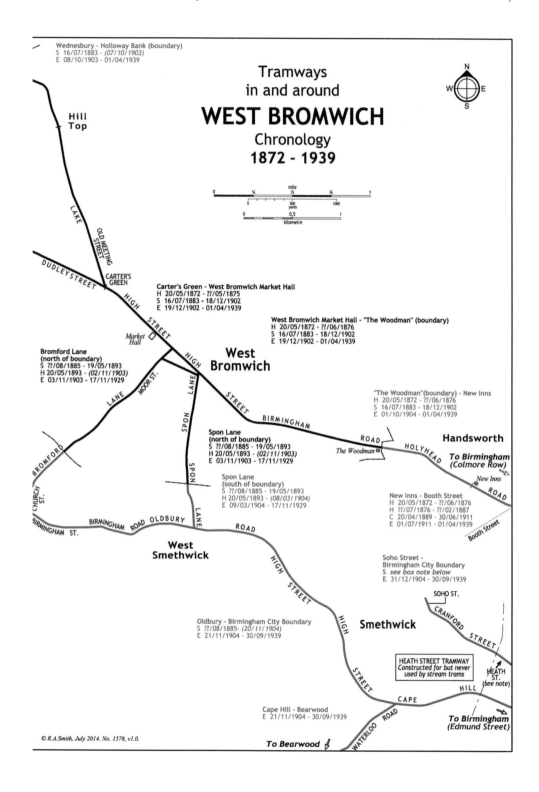

Tramways
in and around
WEST BROMWICH
Chronology
1872 - 1939

Wednesbury - Holloway Bank (boundary)
S 16/07/1883 - (07/10/1903)
E 08/10/1903 - 01/04/1939

Hill Top

Carter's Green - West Bromwich Market Hall
H 20/05/1872 - ??/05/1875
S 16/07/1883 - 18/12/1902
E 19/12/1902 - 01/04/1939

West Bromwich Market Hall - "The Woodman" (boundary)
H 20/05/1872 - ??/06/1876
S 16/07/1883 - 18/12/1902
E 19/12/1902 - 01/04/1939

Market Hall

West Bromwich

Bromford Lane
(north of boundary)
S ??/08/1885 - 19/05/1893
H 20/05/1893 - (02/11/1903)
E 03/11/1903 - 17/11/1929

"The Woodman"(boundary) - New Inns
H 20/05/1872 - ??/06/1876
S 16/07/1883 - 18/12/1902
E 01/10/1904 - 01/04/1939

Handsworth

Spon Lane
(north of boundary)
S ??/08/1885 - 19/05/1893
H 20/05/1893 - (02/11/1903)
E 03/11/1903 - 17/11/1929

The Woodman

To Birmingham
(Colmore Row)

New Inns

Spon Lane
(south of boundary)
S ??/08/1885 - 19/05/1893
H 20/05/1893 - (08/03/1904)
E 09/03/1904 - 17/11/1929

New Inns - Booth Street
H 20/05/1872 - ??/06/1876
H ??/07/1876 - ??/02/1887
C 20/04/1889 - 30/06/1911
E 01/07/1911 - 01/04/1939

Booth Street

West Smethwick

Soho Street -
Birmingham City Boundary
S see box note below
E 31/12/1904 - 30/09/1939

SOHO ST.

Smethwick

Oldbury - Birmingham City Boundary
S ??/08/1885- (20/11/1904)
E 21/11/1904 - 30/09/1939

HEATH STREET TRAMWAY
Constructed for but never
used by stream trams

HEATH ST.
(see note)

Cape Hill - Bearwood
E 21/11/1904 - 30/09/1939

To Birmingham
(Edmund Street)

To Bearwood

© R.A.Smith, July 2014. No. 1578, v1.0.

West Bromwich to Wednesbury and Dudley in the former case, and through Smethwick, Oldbury and Tividale to Dudley on the route operated by the Birmingham & Midlands Tramway Company, which was always known as 'The Track' (see Maps 2 and 3). Put simply, when the running rights in the terms of the lease over the tracks ran out, the trams stopped operating, although with the electrical infrastructure and the steel tramlines in situ, most of the local authorities reluctantly renewed operational rights with BCT in order to get their money's worth out of their capital investment! When urgent renewal of the infrastructure and the expiry date of the operating leases coincided, the faithful trams suddenly became 'old-fashioned', 'in need of replacement' or 'expensive to maintain' and the plethora of local authorities involved in running trams through their District Council area, almost as one, clamoured for the trams to be scrapped in favour of buses.

Both routes succumbed in 1939, with the main line through West Bromwich town centre going on 1 April 1939, when the lease on the former South Staffordshire Tramways route expired and some of the track was in dire need of replacement. This was despite the fact that the routes were nearly always operated by eight-wheel bogie cars with 70 hp motors which were totally enclosed and extremely fast. In the case of the former Birmingham & Midland Tramways-owned Smethwick and Oldbury routes, this occurred despite the outbreak of the Second World War on 3 September 1939, with the closure coming on the last day of that month. Irrespective of the obvious need to reduce the use of fuel oil, all of the Dudley Road routes in Birmingham and those into Smethwick and Oldbury were closed, thus becoming one of the first tram routes in the United Kingdom to be withdrawn after the declaration of war. There was a move to keep the services running within Birmingham and still use some of the large number of redundant 71 Class four-wheeler trams, but this was quickly rejected and the abandonment went ahead anyway.

A Brief History of Tram Operation from 1883 to 1939

The company tramcars operated in West Bromwich belonged to the Birmingham & Midland Tramways Company, who ran on the Bromford and Spon Lane route. This service began with steam trams in August 1885 but these ceased operating in May 1893 and were replaced by Mr Crowther's horse trams. On 3 November 1903, the first sections of both the Bromford Lane and Spon Lane services were electrified, but due to the station bridge at Oldbury Station both routes were only ever operated using single-deckers. The South Staffordshire (Lessee) Company operated double-deck steam trams both from Handsworth to Wednesbury Darlaston from 16 July 1883, and initially to Great Bridge on 14 January 1884, extending this to Dudley on 12 October 1885.

The West Bromwich Corporation Act of 1900 gave the Corporation powers to operate tramcars but only the tramway infrastructure within the borough was purchased by West Bromwich Corporation in 1902. The old steam- and horse-tram routes were then immediately electrified and then leased back to the South Staffordshire Tramways and the Birmingham & Midland Tramways, who supplied and operated their trams over the West Bromwich-owned tracks. On 19 December 1902, the first section of the SST (L) was opened for electric trams between the Handsworth boundary and Carter's Green, which covered all of West Bromwich's high street, with Dudley station being reached on 30 May 1903 and the White Horse at Wednesbury by 8 October 1903. A variety of electric double-deckers were used on both routes. Both the large open-top bogie cars and smaller top-covered four-wheelers found favour through the high street en route for Handsworth at the inner end and Wednesbury, Darlaston and Bilston on one route and Dudley on another; these two services bifurcated at Carter's Green. The B&M Company began operation on 21 November 1904, using open-top, four-wheel, double-deck tramcars, which remained on the route until taken over in 1928 albeit modified by the addition of top-deck covers, new motors and new trucks.

On 31 March 1924, the South Staffordshire lease on the West Bromwich route expired and the service was taken up on a further fifteen-year lease by Birmingham Corporation Tramways, who ran the main-line Birmingham–West Bromwich–Carter's Green–Wednesbury and Great Bridge–Dudley tramcar service until 1 April 1939, when the routes were converted to buses and jointly operated by Birmingham and West Bromwich Corporations. The route through nearby Smethwick to Oldbury and Dudley was transferred to Birmingham operation on 1 April 1928 and abandoned on 30 September 1939, while the Bromford and Spon Lane services were abandoned on 17 November 1929 and operation of West Bromwich Corporation buses began on the following morning.

Midland Metro

Although this book deals specifically with trams in West Bromwich, the long and somewhat tortuous development of the Midland Metro Light Rapid transit system in the West Midlands is worth recounting as it brought trams back to the town.

There are tram stops on the Midland Metro in the West Bromwich area, starting at The Hawthorns. This serves the West Bromwich Albion's football ground and has a platform connection to the Network Railway line which serves Galton Bridge, Blackheath Cradley Heath and Stourbridge. The Hawthorns station is followed by Kenrick Park, Trinity Way and then the main West Bromwich Central interchange opposite the newly refurbished bus station. This is followed by Lodge Road, near to West Bromwich's Town Hall, Dartmouth Street and the Dudley Street, Guns Village station near Carter's Green. The final two stations are at Black Lake, which is located just beyond the only level crossing on the route, and Great Western Street Wednesbury, where the Midland Metro depot is located and where the proposed Line 2 from Wednesbury to the Merry Hill Shopping Centre via Dudley terminates.

The concept of building new tram services radiating from Birmingham had been mooted from the mid-1930s, but it was not until after the cessation of municipal bus operation and the setting up of West Midlands PTE on 1 October 1969 that the possibility of a new network of integrated tram routes became a reality. Routes to Birmingham Airport, Stourbridge and Chelmsley Wood were some of the stillborn suggestions due to either a lack of funding, public opposition and disagreements over route viability. Eventually on 20 June 1984 the pamphlet 'Rapid Transit for the West Midlands' was published and included routes to Sutton Coldfield, Shirley, and Dorridge. The most serious drawback to the scheme was that the first proposed route of the network to Castle Bromwich would have involved the demolition of 238 properties and after a lot of public outcry and opposition, the whole scheme was abandoned in late 1985.

A new West Midlands Passenger Transport Authority was set up in 1986, who suggested proposals for some fifteen new light rapid transit routes to be operated under the present name 'Midland Metro'. On 16 February 1988 WMPTA formally announced that Line 1 would be the first route for Midland Metro operating between Birmingham, Snow Hill and St George's, Wolverhampton, a route not included in the 1984 recommended network. It would use much of the disused track bed of the former Great Western Railway route which had been mothballed by the then Minister of Transport, Mrs Barbara Castle, with a view to reopen the route sometime in the future using much of the existing Victorian infrastructure. On 16 November 1989, the Parliamentary Bill for Line 1 of Midland Metro became an Act and on 31 January 1990 WMPTE was given the brand name 'Centro'.

On 3 August 1995, the contract for the construction of the Metro was signed at a ceremony at the site for The Hawthorns metro station. By this time the estimated construction costs had risen to £145 million, but the concession to design, build and operate the line for a twenty-year period after opening, was given to ALTRAM, a consortium of Ansaldo Transporti and John Laing which had been formed in 1993. West Midlands Travel (Travel Midland Metro) joined in 1996 when this National Express subsidiary later took a 33 per cent share of the ALTRAM consortium. By 2006 the ALTRAM consortium was dissolved and the line became a 100 per cent National Express-owned responsibility through its subsidiary Travel Midland Metro.

In 1997 Centro accepted that they were unable to get funding for any of the proposed new lines, including the much needed Line 2 from Wednesbury to Merry Hill via Dudley, and therefore adopted a strategy of expanding the system in 'bite-sized chunks', with the city-centre extension of Line 1 as the first priority. Construction work for Line 1 began with a JCB digger ceremonially cutting the first sod of turf in the presence of the Transport Secretary, Sir George Young, at a ceremony at West Bromwich on 13 November 1995. Work continued apace along the line and by September 1996 Platform 4 was taken out of use at Snow Hill to be converted as a dead-end platform for the Metro. Construction was completed by the end of 1998 some ten months behind schedule. The first tram to arrive at Wednesbury after being transported from Italy by lowloader via Rotterdam and Immingham was 01 on 17 February 1998, and within two days was shown to the local press and television. The first test run of a Metro tram, on a three mile stretch of track at Wednesbury took place on 16 June and on 3 September 1998 the first tram was tested along the street track in Bilston Road where it reached the Wolverhampton terminus at St George's.

Line 1 of the Midland Metro Line between Birmingham Snow Hill and Wolverhampton St.George's was opened on 31 May 1999 for public service and was formally opened by Princess Anne on September 14th 1999. The 12.5-mile (20.1 km) route between the two cities runs mostly along the track bed of the former Great Western Railway line which had been closed in 1972. It has twenty-three tram stops, eleven of which are former railway stations. Services ran from 06.30 to 23.30 on a basic 10-minute headway requiring twelve of the sixteen trams to be in normal daytime service, with extra trams being operated in the peak periods with a headway of eight minutes. Poor tram reliability was initially a major headache, as was the level of vandalism, so that despite the estimate of eight million passengers per year being carried after a few years this had stabilised to barely 5.5 million passengers per year. The southern end the terminus is at Birmingham's Snow Hill station, using Platform 4 which allows interchange with the National Rail network. From Snow Hill, the line runs north-west along the old Great Western railway line and for the first few miles it runs alongside Network Rail's Birmingham to Worcester railway line, before the two diverge. On this section the Jewellery Quarter and The Hawthorns stations are tram/railway interchange points.

On 12 December 2000, Government approval was given for Metro Line 2 from Wednesbury to the Merry Hill Centre and Brierley Hill via Dudley port and Dudley. Despite road bridge strengthening on numerous bridges over the long-abandoned track bed of the former Great Western Railway line, funding has never been forthcoming and promises, proposals and procrastination over a twenty-year period have resulted in not a rail being laid. This important link across the Black Country is vital for future economic development in the area but still remains an optimistic dream.

The fact that the existing line did not run into Birmingham city centre was identified as one of the reasons why the Midland Metro has consistently failed to carry the predicted number of passengers. An order authorising the Birmingham City Centre Extension was made in July 2005 which would link Snow Hill station to New Street station by a street tramway. This Birmingham City Centre Extension extends Line 1 into the streets of central Birmingham leaving Snow Hill, where the present Platform 4 terminus will be abandoned. The Metro tramway runs along Colmore Circus, Upper Bull Street, and Corporation Street with three stops. Originally it was planned to terminate the extension at Stephenson Street, adjacent to New Street railway station, but a second extension phase was applied for and Government approval was given on 16 February 2012 for the extension, a new fleet of trams and a new depot at Wednesbury. The sanctioned sum is £128 million, of which £75.4 million will be provided by the Department for Transport. On 14 June 2012 works on the extension officially began. Initial works include the relocation of underground services on Bull Street and Corporation Street.

In September 2013, Centro started consultation on proposals to extend the city-centre extension from New Street station to Centenary Square via Pinfold Street, Victoria Square, Paradise Street and Broad Street, with an additional stop at Birmingham Town Hall. This would be another of the 'bite-sized' extensions that would enable the trams to reach the original destination at Five Ways. The first new CAF Urbos 3 trams came into service on the existing line in September 2014, stabled at the newly enlarged Wednesbury depot. The extension as far as New Street station and the full new tram fleet are scheduled to be in service from March 2015, with the further extension to Centenary Square in operation from 2017.

At the northern end of the line, the tram route leaves the former railway track bed at Priestfield to run along Bilston Road to the St George's terminus in Wolverhampton's city centre at Bilston Street. An extension along Piper's Row from near the existing St George's terminus with two new stops opposite the bus station and the terminus at Wolverhampton railway station is due to be completed at the end of 2015.

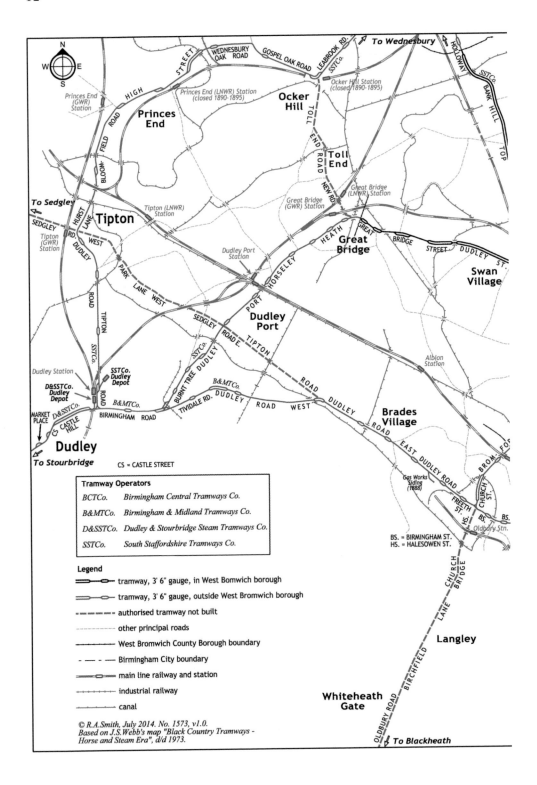

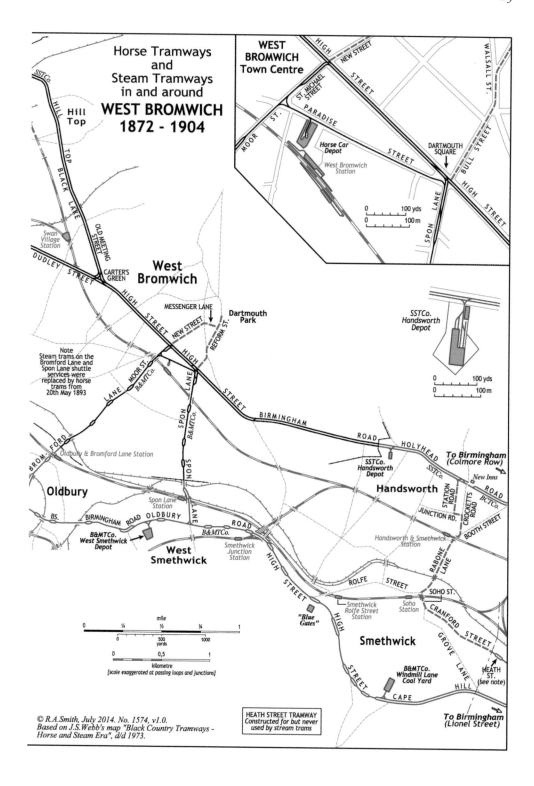

Horse Tramways
and
Steam Tramways
in and around
**WEST BROMWICH
1872 - 1904**

WEST
BROMWICH
Town Centre

Hill
Top

SSTCo.

HILL TOP

BLACK LANE

OLD MEETING STREET

Swan
Village
Station

DUDLEY STREET

CARTER'S
GREEN

**West
Bromwich**

MESSENGER LANE

HIGH STREET

NEW STREET

REFORM ST.

Dartmouth
Park

Note
Steam trams on the
Bromford Lane and
Spon Lane shuttle
services were
replaced by horse
trams from
20th May 1893

MOOR ST.

B&MTCo.

LANE

SPON LANE

B&MTCo.

HIGH STREET

BIRMINGHAM

BROMFORD

Oldbury & Bromford Lane Station

SPON LANE

ROAD

HOLYHEAD

SSTCo.
Handsworth
Depot

To Birmingham
(Colmore Row)

New Inns

ROAD

BCTCo.

Oldbury

BS.

BIRMINGHAM ROAD OLDBURY

Spon Lane
Station

SPON LANE

ROAD

B&MTCo.

Handsworth

STATION ROAD

CROCKETTS ROAD

JUNCTION RD.

BOOTH STREET

B&MTCo.
West Smethwick
Depot

**West
Smethwick**

Smethwick
Junction
Station

HIGH STREET

Handsworth & Smethwick
Station

RABONE LANE

ROLFE STREET

SOHO ST.

Smethwick
Rolfe Street
Station

Soho
Station

CRANFORD STREET

"Blue
Gates"

HIGH STREET

Smethwick

GROVE LANE

HEATH ST.
(see note)

STREET

B&MTCo.
Windmill Lane
Coal Yard

HILL

CAPE

To Birmingham
(Lionel Street)

mile
0   ¼   ½   ¾   1

0   500   1000
yards

0   0,5   1
kilometre
[scale exaggerated at passing loops and junctions]

© R.A.Smith, July 2014. No. 1574, v1.0.
Based on J.S.Webb's map "Black Country Tramways -
Horse and Steam Era", d/d 1973.

HEATH STREET TRAMWAY
Constructed for but never
used by stream trams

Inset — West Bromwich Town Centre:

WEST
BROMWICH
Town Centre

HIGH STREET

NEW STREET

WALSALL ST.

ST. MICHAEL
STREET

PARADISE

STREET

MOOR ST.

Horse Car
Depot

West Bromwich
Station

STREET

DARTMOUTH
SQUARE

BULL STREET

HIGH STREET

SPON LANE

0   100 yds
0   100m

SSTCo.
Handsworth
Depot

0   100 yds
0   100m

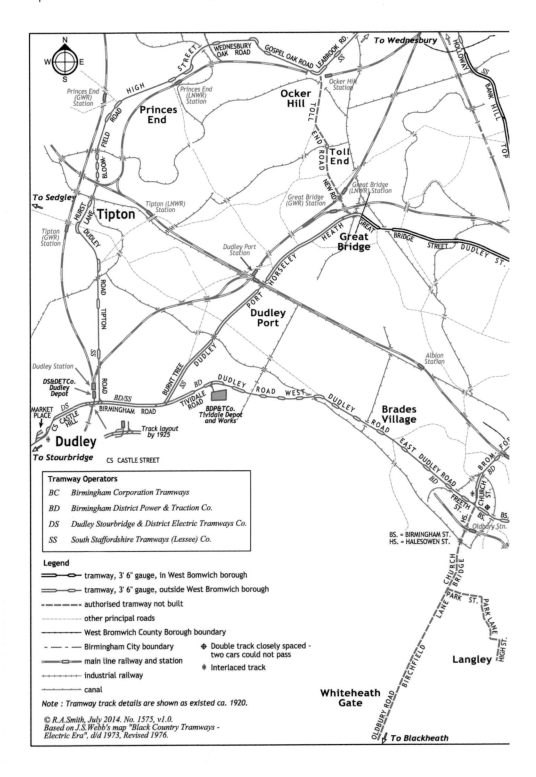

Tramway Operators

BC	Birmingham Corporation Tramways
BD	Birmingham District Power & Traction Co.
DS	Dudley Stourbridge & District Electric Tramways Co.
SS	South Staffordshire Tramways (Lessee) Co.

Legend

- tramway, 3' 6" gauge, in West Bromwich borough
- tramway, 3' 6" gauge, outside West Bromwich borough
- authorised tramway not built
- other principal roads
- West Bromwich County Borough boundary
- Birmingham City boundary
- main line railway and station
- industrial railway
- canal

⊕ Double track closely spaced - two cars could not pass

✶ Interlaced track

Note : Tramway track details are shown as existed ca. 1920.

© R.A.Smith, July 2014. No. 1575, v1.0.
Based on J.S.Webb's map "Black Country Tramways -
Electric Era", d/d 1973, Revised 1976.

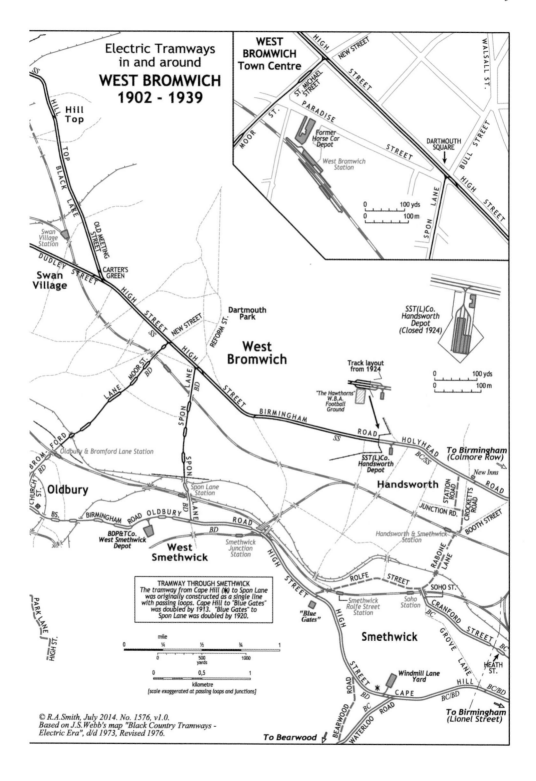

Electric Tramways
in and around
WEST BROMWICH
1902 - 1939

WEST BROMWICH Town Centre

Former Horse Car Depot

West Bromwich Station

DARTMOUTH SQUARE

SST(L)Co. Handsworth Depot (Closed 1924)

Track layout from 1924

"The Hawthorns" W.B.A. Football Ground

SST(L)Co. Handsworth Depot

To Birmingham (Colmore Row)

New Inns

Hill Top

Swan Village Station

CARTER'S GREEN

Swan Village

Dartmouth Park

West Bromwich

Oldbury & Bromford Lane Station

Oldbury

Spon Lane Station

Handsworth

Handsworth & Smethwick Station

BDP&TCo. West Smethwick Depot

West Smethwick

Smethwick Junction Station

Smethwick Rolfe Street Station

Soho Station

TRAMWAY THROUGH SMETHWICK
The tramway from Cape Hill (✳) to Spon Lane
was originally constructed as a single line
with passing loops. Cape Hill to "Blue Gates"
was doubled by 1913. "Blue Gates" to
Spon Lane was doubled by 1920.

"Blue Gates"

Smethwick

Windmill Lane Yard

HEATH ST.

mile
0   ¼   ½   ¾   1

0   500   1000
yards

0   0,5   1
kilometre
[scale exaggerated at passing loops and junctions]

To Birmingham (Lionel Street)

© R.A.Smith, July 2014. No. 1576, v1.0.
Based on J.S.Webb's map "Black Country Tramways -
Electric Era", d/d 1973, Revised 1976.

To Bearwood

The Main-Line Route from Birmingham to Wednesbury and Dudley via Carter's Green Operated by South Staffordshire Tramways Co. Ltd and Birmingham Corporation Tramways

South Staffordshire Tramways (Lessee) Co. Ltd

18.3 miles operated, of which 6.86 owned, including 5.23 for West Bromwich, 3.7 for Wednesbury and 0.79 for Dudley.

'Main line', operated by Birmingham Corporation from 1 April 1924 to 1 April 1939.

Livery reddish brown, later Munich Lake and cream, finally Corinthian green and cream.

It is easier to examine this service from one end to the other during the South Staffordshire (Lessee) period of company car operation until 1924, and then the 1924 to 1939 period when operated by Birmingham Corporation Tramway's Department. Many of these photographs have appeared elsewhere as there is only a limited number of photographs of SS and BCT trams on the routes through West Bromwich.

Birmingham to Handsworth
Car 542
The Birmingham terminus for the West Bromwich tram services was in front of Snow Hill station in Colmore Row. Car 542, a UEC-built bogie tram built in 1913 and mounted on Mountain & Gibson bogies, has stopped at the top of Livery Street at the Birmingham boundary in Holyhead Road when working on the 23 service to 'The Hawthorns' in about 1920. The tram is still in its original open-balcony state, as work on enclosing the balconies of the whole of the 512 Class did not begin until May 1926. (Commercial Postcard)

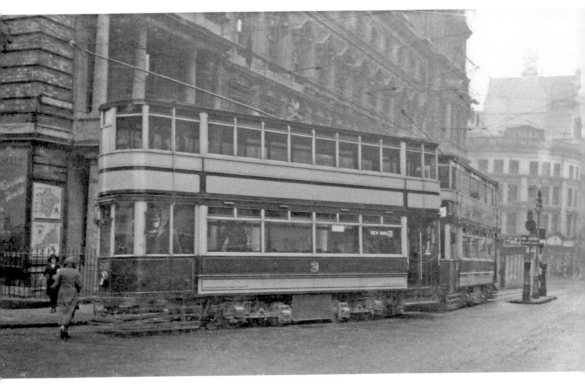

SS 6 *(Opposite above)*
A South Staffordshire (Lessee) tramcar stands in Livery Street, Birmingham, alongside the refreshment and dining rooms of the Great Western Hotel in about 1920. Open-balcony, four-wheeled Car 6 was built during the First World War by Birmingham & Midland at their Tividale Works and had a Brush flexible truck and a seating capacity of forty-eight. Car 6 is working on the Black Country through car service, which was inaugurated on 9 October 1912 to Darlaston, though the use of the line forming a loop which included Livery Street was not brought into use until 13 June 1913. Between the decks the tram is carrying the legend 'West Bromwich, Wednesbury and Darlaston'. After 26 May 1923 the route was extended, with every other tram going to Bilston. (D. R. Harvey Collection)

527 *(Opposite below)*
Halfway around the curve from Livery Street into Colmore Row in about 1933 is Car 527. It has pulled up behind another bogie car working on one of the services through West Bromwich, which is standing outside the main entrance to Snow Hill station. Car 527, a UEC-bodied tram delivered in November 1913 and mounted on M & G Burnley-type maximum-traction bogies, was on its third different type of motor by this time, having been fitted with GEC WT 32R 70 hp motors in 1927. In this photograph it is being used on the 29 route short working to the New Inns. (D. R. Harvey Collection)

Car 587 *(Above)*
On Friday 31 March 1939, Hockley Brook was still an important mid-Victorian shopping centre but was totally swept away when Hockley flyover was built in the 1970s. A line of trams, led by Car 587, has descended Soho Hill and is crossing the junction with Farm Street on its way towards the city on the 74 service from Dudley and West Bromwich. To the left are the tracks leading into Whitmore Street and to Hockley depot. In the distance can be seen the tram-stop shelter built in 1935 in the middle of the junction with Claremont Road. The policeman on point duty is allowing the main-road traffic to have priority. In the distance is a 1938 EOG-registered Daimler COG5 working into the city on the 15 bus route. (H. B. Priestley)

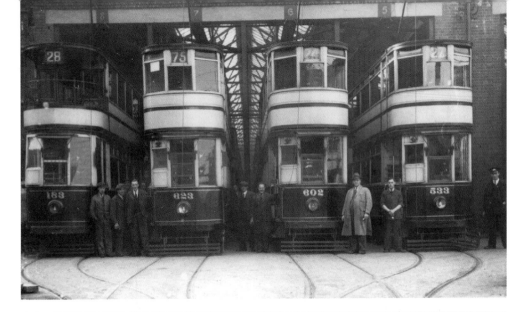

183, 623, 602, 533 *(Top)*

The trams operated by Birmingham Corporation Tramways after 1 April 1924 for the West Bromwich 'main-line' services were stabled at Hockley depot. Parked at the entrance to rows 5–7 are three of the standard bogie cars allocated to Hockley depot as well as an older four-wheel, open-balconied tram parked in row 8. This was Car 183, which was one of just four 71 Class trams used for peak-time extras. Tram 533 is a pre-First World War UEC-built tram mounted on M & G Burnley maximum traction bogies and re-motored with a pair of GEC WT32R 70 hp units in August 1927. Cars 602 and 623 were built by Brush in 1921 and were re-motored in 1928 with DK 30/1L 63 hp motors. Car 623 was later to become the penultimate Birmingham tram when used in the closing ceremony on 4 July 1953. Staff from the depot take the opportunity to pose in front of

the row of tramcars on 29 March 1939, three days before the Soho Road routes were abandoned. Immediately before the trams were abandoned in April 1939, Hockley depot had an allocation of 110 trams. (W. A. Camwell)

128 *(Opposite below)*
The tramcar used to close the Soho Road routes to West Bromwich and Dudley was former Radial-trucked, UEC-bodied Car 128. This tram nominally operated as a 73 service, starting in Carter's Green. Car 551 was the last tram to Wednesbury, and on its return to Carter's Green its passengers were transferred to the elderly and about-to-be-scrapped 128. Meanwhile, 551 returned to Dudley and in darkness went to Selly Oak depot via the West Smethwick route. This was one of the twenty-one Hockley bogie cars which went to their new depots via 'the Track'. Car 128 is travelling along Whitmore Street in its final moments of glory – by the time it returned to Hockley depot in the early hours of Sunday 2 April 1939 it had been stripped of nearly every unscrewable souvenir. Not surprisingly, 128 was taken to West Smethwick depot, where Cashmores broke it up two months later. (D. R. Harvey Collection)

230 *(Above)*
On Saturday 1 July 1911, electric trams replaced the CBT cable cars from Birmingham through Handsworth UDC to the New Inns. UEC-bodied, Brill-trucked Car 230 has just returned from the Handsworth boundary. It carries an advertisement for Holders Stout, which was brewed in Nova Scotia Street; Ashted and Cheshire's Brewery, which licensed the Frighted Horse pub immediately behind the tram, were both taken over by Mitchells & Butlers. Car 225 is passing a cross-over that had been laid into the old cable track to enable cars to turn back at Stafford Road; the cable conduit can be seen between the lines. In the distance is the two-month-old top-covered car 324. (D. R. Harvey Collection)

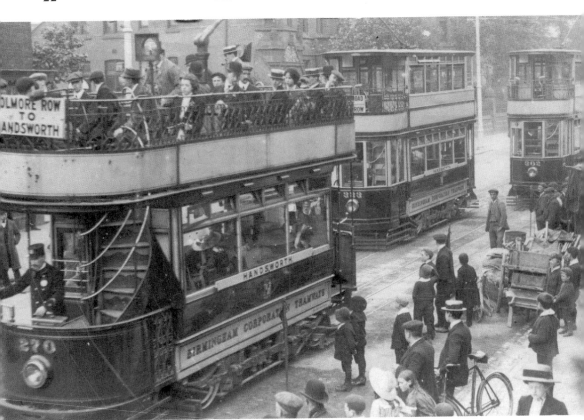

Soho Road.

270 *(Opposite above)*

A crowd of people stand watching the passage of the new cars as they cross in Soho Road at Handsworth Council House on 1 July 1911. Fiercely independent of Birmingham's influence, Handsworth had been in Staffordshire and regarded itself as part of the Black Country. The foundation stone of the Council House was laid on 30 October 1877, but this example of civic pride was to lead a truncated life in its original role after the UDC was incorporated into Birmingham. UEC-bodied open-top tram 270, mounted on a 6-foot wheelbase Brill 21E truck dating from May 1907, is travelling past the Frighted Horse public house on its way from Colmore Row to Handsworth. Behind this tram are two empty, new top-covered UEC-bodied tramcars, 333 and 302. (D. R. Harvey collection)

614 *(Opposite below)*

Car 614 leaves the Soho Road junction with Grove Lane after turning towards the city when working the 26 route from Oxhill Road. In the background, the tower of Handsworth Council House dominates the skyline, while the row of buildings along Soho Road has not yet been totally converted to retail use. This was the heart of Soho Road's shopping centre and was the last retail area before West Bromwich was reached. The double-fronted early Victorian house, just behind the last two children crossing the main road, is still protected by a small brick wall surmounted by iron railings; it was later converted into a Westminster Bank. (Commercial Postcard)

236 *(Above)*

When the Handsworth tram route was taken over by Birmingham Corporation on 1 July 1911, most of the trams used were members of the 221 Class of open-top tramcars built by UEC on Brill 21E 6-foot wheelbase trucks. These trams were operated from the Miller Street Depot until June 1912, when the conversion of Hockley Depot from cable to electric tram operation was completed. Travelling from the New Inns in Holyhead Road is Car 236, dating from April 1907. Soon after the takeover by BCT in the late summer of 1911, the tram is having to use the old cable car tracks as well as negotiating the horse droppings on the road surface. The sagging overhead is a most unusual feature for tramcar operations by BCT! (D. R. Harvey Collection)

New Inns to The Hawthorns
South Staffordshire 62
Leaving the New Inns, whose lanterns are just visible behind the trees to the right of the tramcar, is South Staffordshire Car 62. It is on its way to Colmore Row and Snow Hill Station when working on a Black Country Through Car service from Darlaston. Car 62 was built in early 1916 by the B&M at Tividale Works and was designed to be the new standard double-deck tramcar for all the Black Country operators, with enclosed platforms that gave permanent protection for the driver. The bodies, incorporating some structural parts manufactured by Brush, sat twenty-six passengers in the upper saloon and twenty-two downstairs and were mounted on second-hand Brush-built Lycett & Conaty 8-foot 6-inch trucks. These had a rather long wheelbase and were formerly radial trucks which were locked up but made flexible in order to get around sharp curves, though the rather rigid ride of these trams would not have been made any better by the state of the tram track, which was in dire need of replacement. (D. R. Harvey Collection)

64

Standing in Holyhead Road is BCT Car 64. It is working on the 28 route and is outside the New Inns, Handsworth, with its prominent clock. This was the original CBT cable tram terminus from Birmingham. After the opening of the Corporation electric service on 1 July 1911, the 28 service became a shortworking of the 23 route to the West Bromwich boundary. Corporation Car 64 was one of the Brill 21E-trucked cars built by UEC in 1905. It was rebuilt with a top cover and Maley track brakes before the First World War. In the distant Holyhead Road is a South Staffordshire Company 'Aston' type four-wheel tramcar, identifiable by its triangular screen beneath the vestibule window. It is working the Black Country Through Service from Darlaston to Colmore Row, dating this view to before April 1924, when BCT took over the West Bromwich routes. (Commercial Postcard)

CBT cable car *(Top)*

The terminus of the CBT cable cars was the New Inns, Handsworth, on the corner of Sandwell Road and Crocketts Lane. This was the second half of the route from Birmingham and was opened from Hockley on 20 April 1889. Although neither of the two cable cars is identifiable, the one on the right is one of the 1888 Falcon-built trams, while the tram on the left is a 1902-vintage CBT-built tram. The New Inns, a Mitchells &

The New Inns, Handsworth.

Butlers-owned public house, in this form, was not opened until 1901, when it replaced a much older inn. The interior of the New Inns was decorated with Art Nouveau ceramic tiles and its opulence made it a prime venue for weddings and other important functions. In the distance, on the other side of Crocketts Road, are two South Staffordshire open-top electric bogie trams. (Commercial Postcard)

Car 536 and 541 *(Opposite below)*

Standing in Holyhead Road, just short of the junction with Sandwell Road at the New Inns, on 7 September 1938 is UEC Car 536, which is travelling towards Birmingham on the 75 route. The trams are waiting outside Lloyds Bank, which was set back from the main road. On the tram standard are a number of signposts, the top one reading 'Smethwick 1½' (miles). In front of 536 is Tram 541, another one of the same class, which is on the 28 shortworking to the New Inns from the city centre. The car in front of the second tram is a large Austin 18 saloon. The New Inns public house was built for Mitchell & Butlers in 1901, though its huge Assembly Room was not finished until 1904. The interior was decorated with Art Nouveau ceramic tiles and was regarded as being one of the gems of interior public house design in the Birmingham area. The pub had been derelict for many years but was largely saved and was converted to flats at the end of November 1995. (R. T. Wilson)

South Staffordshire 14 *(Above)*

One of the large seventy-seat Brush-bodied bogie cars, dating from 1902, stands at the New Inns on the Handsworth UDC boundary. The South Staffordshire (Lessee) Company tram, 14, is preparing to leave for Dudley by way of West Bromwich. On 11 September 1909, this tram ran away down Holyhead Road and collided with a cable car due to the electric tram having a defective track brake – it should not have even left the depot at The Hawthorns. This tram was one of seven of the 10-27 Class that was cut down to a single-deck for use on the Dudley–Tipton–Wednesbury service, on which there was a low bridge in Bloomfield Road, Tipton. Behind it are two CBT cable trams working on the service via Hockley into Birmingham. (Commercial Postcard)

South Staffordshire 40

Travelling along Holyhead Road towards The New Inns is South Staffordshire tram 40. It is working on a Through Car service to Birmingham. This 'Aston'-type double-deck radial truck car had been built by Brush for the Birmingham & Midland Tramways in 1904, but was one of fifteen transferred to the South Staffordshire system in 1907 and fitted with a top cover some two years later. The tram has also been fitted with a platform driver's screen. (Commercial Postcard)

Around The Hawthorns

South Staffordshire 13

Handsworth depot in Holyhead Road, was originally constructed for the South Staffordshire steam trams and opened on 16 July 1883. It was converted for storing a maximum of four large bogie electric trams on 20 December 1902. It was not wired for electric trams until the extension from The Hawthorns to the New Inns was opened on 1 October 1904. During this interim period the trams were towed in and out of the depot by a steam tram, in this case one of the Wilkinson Patent vertical boiler locomotives built by Beyer Peacock. The depot was next to West Bromwich Albion's Hawthorns Football ground and after 1906 was only used to park tramcars on match days. The tram is Car 13, one of the eighteen members of the 10-27 Class of large Brush open-top, five-windowed, seventy-seat bogie trams delivered to South Staffordshire around the cusp of 1902 and 1903. They were fitted on reversed Brush B type reversed maximum traction bogies, with the small pony wheels leading. This was in order to allow sufficient clearance under the platform bearers when negotiating sharp curves, but in reality led to the regular derailment of the pony wheels as the advantage of having up to 80 per cent of the tram's weight was lost. Car 13 would only remain a double-decker until about 1912, when it became one of the five class members to be cut down to single-decker format in order to work on the Dudley–Tipton–Wednesbury line and was withdrawn in 1917. (D. R. Harvey Collection)

Car 562, 540 *(Top)*

25 March 1939 was the last home fixture played by West Bromwich Albion at The Hawthorns to be served by Birmingham's trams. The 'Baggies' were playing Fulham in the Second Division Championship and won 3-0. Parked in the Hawthorns depot in Holyhead Road in front of the Vauxhall Light Six 12 are two UEC-bodied bogie trams from 1914, specifically cars 562 and 540. Both trams had been re-motored in 1926 with Dick, Kerr DK30/ 1L 63 hp motors and also had their balconies enclosed about the same time. Car 562 would survive until the penultimate day of tramcar operation in Birmingham on 3 July 1953, whereas 540 went after the closure of the Washwood Heath service and was broken up in November 1950. Parked in the distant Holyhead Road are some of the BCT buses used to take supporters to locations in Birmingham not directly accessible by tram. By the time of the next home game on 8 April against Millwall, the buses had taken over. (D. Clayton)

Car 598, 553 (*Opposite below*)
The small Albion depot on the Handsworth boundary in Holyhead Road was built by the South Staffordshire Tramways Company, supplying trams for the West Bromwich, Dudley and Darlaston services. After 1924 it was used only as parking space for up to eight trams when West Bromwich Albion were playing at home at the nearby Hawthorns ground. The stores van, 6, which spent most of its life at Hockley depot, would be driven up to the Albion depot on match days and used to supply conductors with new stocks of tickets. This van, mounted on Mountain & Gibson 21E trucks, had been the last of six built in January 1907 for general department uses. When Hockley depot closed, Van 6 went into storage and was broken up in 1945. In March 1939 some of the platform staff pose in front of UEC-bodied Car 553 and Brush-bodied Car 598. Albion depot closed on 2 April 1939 and the premises were converted to industrial use. After fifty years Albion depot was rebuilt at the Black Country Living Museum in Dudley as the museum's tram depot. (D. R. Harvey Collection)

Car 521 (*Above*)
The Hawthorns football ground, home of West Bromwich Albion, not only had the distinction of being the highest Football League ground in England and Scotland at 551 feet above sea level, but was the only place on the Birmingham Corporation tramway system to have four parallel tramlines. On the right Car 521, a rebuilt UEC-built totally enclosed 70 hp bogie car, heads a line of trams facing Birmingham during 1938, while Brush-bodied bogie Car 615 on the left is at the back of the line of trams going to West Bromwich on the Hawthorns football side of Holyhead Road. The long lines of trams are parked on the kerbside tracks which left the two middle lines for normal tram services. Just visible on the left above the tramcar roofs is the Woodman public house, which marked the Birmingham–West Bromwich boundary and where both tram and the later bus passengers had to rebook in order to continue their journey. (W. A. Camwell)

Car 59, 514 *(Opposite above)*
Sometime before it was transferred from Hockley to Rosebery Street depot on 22 May
1935, UEC-bodied Brill 21E trucked Car 59, fitted with the Maley track brake, stands
at the rear of the line of West Bromwich football specials facing Birmingham. This tram
should have a bow collector for use on the tortuous Lodge Road, but it is not clear if it has
been so fitted. These Brill-Maley forty-eight-seaters were generally used by this time for
peak hour extras, shortworkings and, obviously, football specials. On the opposite side of
Birmingham Road and parked alongside the Hawthorns brick wall is 1913 UEC-bodied
bogie Car 514, which had recently had its balconies enclosed. (D. R. Harvey Collection)

Car 182 *(Opposite below)*
Saturday 23 October 1937 was not a good day for West Bromwich Albion. They played
Sunderland at the Hawthorns and lost 6-1. Perhaps going to the Birmingham University
Hospital Carnival, as advertised on the fender of Car 182, might have been a better bet!
Car 182, facing Birmingham, one of the former radial trucked, UEC-bodied 71 Class
trams had only been allocated to Hockley depot since 27 January and would be moved
just over a year later for a brief sojourn at Coventry Road. These elderly trams were used
in the peak periods, leaving the all-day services to the more powerful bogie cars. These
71 Class trams were the obvious choice for scrapping since the majority had non-standard
or low-powered equipment and motors while the bodies were of high-bridge construction,
thus restricting their range of operation. (W. A. Camwell)

Cars 617, 548, 621 *(Above)*
The roof of the Woodman public house stands above the row of trams, led by Car 548,
lined up outside the outer wall of the Hawthorns. It is 25 March 1939 and with only a
week before the tram routes through West Bromwich would be abandoned, the notices
of the changeover to buses are already in the windows of the trams. None of Hockley's
large bogie cars would be withdrawn because of this closure but it led to the withdrawal,
directly or indirectly, of some thirty-three ex-Radial Class cars in April 1939. The football
specials were lined up on the kerbsides, leaving the two centre tracks for the normal
service cars. (D. C. Clayton)

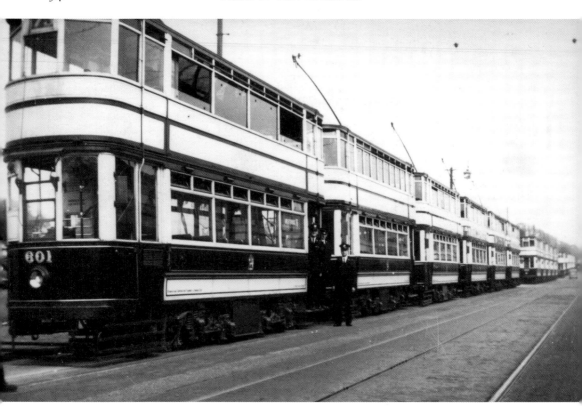

601 *(Opposite above)*
Looking back towards Handsworth and Birmingham, opposite the Hawthorns football ground, is Car 601. This 1920-vintage Brush-bodied tram originally had open balconies but these were enclosed in the late 1920s. It was transferred from Moseley Road depot to Hockley when it was just four years old and this provided the tram with its longest period of stability as it remained working on the West Bromwich routes until those routes were closed on 1 April 1939. It is parked at the back of a row of approximately sixteen tramcars on a football special working on 27 August 1938. This was the first match of the 1938/39 season and this was against Luton Town, who were beaten by West Bromwich Albion 3-0. (D. R. Harvey Collection)

631 *(Opposite below)*
On a rainy match day the 'Baggies' supporters begin to stream away from the ground in order to catch trams heading for Handsworth and Birmingham. Apparently being ignored is Car 631, a Brush-bodied totally enclosed bogie, which is standing outside the M&B-owned Woodman Public House in Birmingham Road, facing West Bromwich, in the shadow of The Hawthorns. The tram is working on the 73 short working to Carter's Green. Car 631 would survive until November 1950, when it was one of twenty-six trams from these 1920-built trams to be declared redundant. (J. S. Webb)

543 *(Above)*
The 77 service to Spon Lane could be operated either from the Birmingham end of the route or from either Dudley or Wednesbury via Carter's Green. The terminus was realistically Dartmouth Square end of the high street in West Bromwich, and perhaps might have been confused with the abandoned Birmingham & Midland Tramways single-deck tram service to the Spon Croft. A rather smart-looking Car 543, a 70 hp bogie car rebuilt about twelve years earlier with new motors, totally enclosed balconies and fitted with upholstered seating, stands on the through track to West Bromwich outside the Woodman Public House on 1 April 1939. (L. W. Perkins)

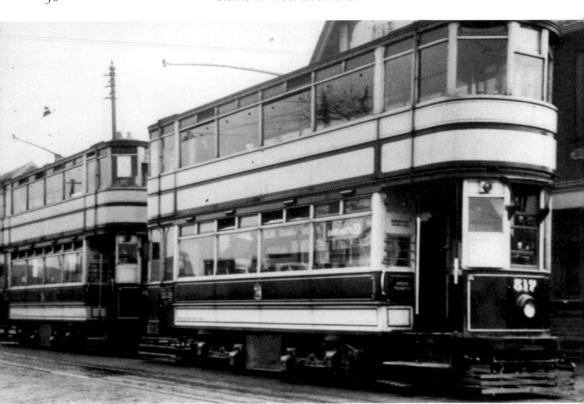

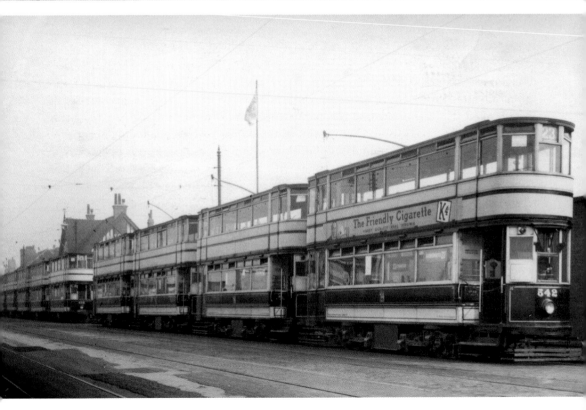

517 *(Opposite above)*

The Woodman Public House was in Holyhead Road, just before it became Birmingham Road at the eastern end of the Hawthorns football ground. Parked in the kerbside tracks outside the hostelry, facing West Bromwich, on 1 April 1939 is UEC-bodied bogie Car 517. It has arrived from Birmingham on a 23 service, but as it is facing West Bromwich and is parked on the tracks used for the Football Specials, the destination blinds have yet to be changed. Behind it is Brush-bodied bogie Car 609, working on the 77 route to Dartmouth Square/Spon Lane. (L. W. Perkins)

542 *(Opposite below)*

On Saturday 1 April 1939, the 'Baggies' reserves were playing at home, but, despite the comparative unimportance of the match, no less than ten eight-wheeled trams are waiting alongside the Hawthorns in Birmingham Road with the Woodman Public House in the background. The rest of the first group of trams are 514, 517 and 636. The leading tram of the second group is Car 616, which was destined to become Birmingham's last tram on 4 July 1953. The leading tram, Brush Burnley bogie Car 542, had its balconies enclosed in December 1926 and was re-seated in April 1932 to be a sixty-one-seater. This was the last day of tramcar operation to West Bromwich, though most of the supporters wouldn't have noticed until the next home game, when a few might have noticed that their vehicle home was a bus. (L. W. Perkins)

Car 609 *(Above)*

On Saturday 25 March 1939 the 'Baggies' played Fulham at The Hawthorns and won the match 3-0. This was their first season back in the Football League's Second Division, having been relegated in 1938. At the end of the 1938/39 season, they finished tenth in the division. Brush-bodied bogie Car 609 is working on the 73 route from Carter's Green as it passes the football supporters going to the game. Car 609 would survive until the penultimate day of tram operation in Birmingham and be broken up by Friday 17 July 1953 at Witton depot. (D. Clayton)

Car 565

On 31 March 1939, UEC-bodied Car 565 speeds across the long, flat, straight section of the tram route from the distant Hawthorns towards West Bromwich when working the 75 route to Wednesbury. This was a section of route on which the trams could be notched-up and really exhibit the performance available to the higher-horsepower cars. This 63 hp tram was probably more than a match for the small Thornycroft lorry it is overtaking. The area to the right at this time was largely undeveloped, while to the left was the home of Dartmouth Cricket Club, for many years a major force in Birmingham League cricket. (H. B. Priestley)

High Street, West Bromwich

South Staffordshire Tramways Co. Ltd Loco 3

Once across the Sandwell Valley, Birmingham Road became High Street just before Roebuck Lane. Here, large gabled villas and terraces had been built in the last decade of the nineteenth century as the town expanded eastwards towards Birmingham. This expansion was indirectly encouraged by the opening on 16 July 1883 of the Handsworth (New Inns), West Bromwich, Wednesbury and Darlaston steam tram service of the South Staffordshire & Birmingham District Steam Tramways Co. Ltd. The combination of Beyer, Peacock steam tram loco number 3, built in 1883, and one of the large Starbuck sixty-seat trailers must have been an impressive sight as it hissed along its route. The tram is passing Bagnall Street in about 1900. The turreted house on the extreme left of the photograph still stands, although the steam trams on this section of the route were withdrawn on 19 December 1902 and replaced by South Staffordshire electric cars. (D. R. Harvey Collection)

South Staffordshire Tram *(Opposite above)*
An unidentified open-top, double-deck tram belonging to the South Staffordshire Tramways (Lessee) Company passes the junction with Thynne Street as it travels towards the Handsworth boundary. Hidden by the tramcar is the Edwardian police station, while in the distance is Dartmouth Square and the junction with both Spon Lane and Paradise Street. There are lots of young boys in the street, but with the exception of one distant horse and cart there is no other vehicular traffic, though there is recent evidence to the contrary just in front of the tram. (Commercial Postcard)

South Staffordshire Tram Conversion *(Opposite below)*
On 19 December 1902, the first section of the South Staffordshire (Lessee) Company's electric tram service from The Woodman Inn at the Handsworth boundary, adjacent to West Bromwich Albion FC's Hawthorns football ground, to Carter's Green was opened. The through route to Wednesbury was opened on 8 October 1903, while the service via Great Bridge to Dudley was electrified on 30 May 1903. The link through Handsworth to meet the CBT cable trams at The New Inns, however, wasn't completed until 1 October 1904 due to legal wrangles. But that was nearly two years away when this first section of electrified route was opened with due ceremony. At Dartmouth Square, the old met the new. One of Mr Crowther's later horse trams, a South Staffordshire Beyer Peacock steam locomotive and a Falcon double-deck trailer were posed in front of the Bull's Head public house on the corner of Spon Lane with one of the new open-top five-bay double-deck bogie cars built by Brush of Loughborough and mounted on Brush A type reversed maximum traction bogies in late 1902. They were numbered 10–27. (D. R. Harvey Collection)

Dartmouth Square *(Above)*
In the distance, an open-top South Staffordshire tram travels towards Dartmouth Square in about 1913 as the ornamental fountain has been replaced by the clock. To the left, partially masked by the mothers with their perambulators, is Paradise Street and between the two are the premises of Broadhead's Bakery and tea rooms, which occupied the site for over sixty years. The state of the track in High Street looks in need of some attention and must have given a fairly uncomfortable ride on the trams as they passed over the points taking trams into Spon Lane. (Commercial Postcard)

DARTMOUTH SQUARE, WEST BROMWICH.

South Staffordshire 5 *(Top)*

ER&TCW 'Baltimore' tram number 5 was intended to be a single-decker but was rebuilt as an open-top double-decker before it was delivered in 1902. There were only three of these trams, which had reversed stairs, Lord Baltimore trucks and a pair of 25 hp Walker motors. They had a seating capacity of twenty-six inside and twenty-five on the top deck. Car 5 is passing along High Street at Dartmouth Square in about 1905 and is passing on the left the ornamental cast-iron drinking fountain erected in 1885 by Reuben Farley, who was the first mayor of West Bromwich, in memory of his recently deceased mother. It is working on a short working to Great Bridge. These trams had comparatively short lives, being withdrawn by 1913. (D. R. Harvey Collection)

South Staffordshire 15 *(Opposite below)*

The boy conductor on the platform of the South Staffordshire Company bogie tramcar looks on somewhat apprehensively as a company inspector checks his waybill. In those days cash errors would be docked from the conductor's wages, while any excess money would go to the company. It was a ruthless system as there was only one winner and the conductor could be dismissed. Car 15 was one of eighteen large, open-topped bogie cars built by Brush in late 1902. They were not long-lived trams, with 15 being one of the last seven in service; it was scrapped in 1924. The tram is on its way to Wednesbury around 1908 before the unusual and elaborately designed, centrally mounted traction poles in High Street, West Bromwich, were replaced by the more usual span wiring. (Commercial Postcard)

South Staffordshire Bogie Car 10-27 *(Above)*

Just ten seconds more and the identity of this tram would have been known! Another of the 10-27 Class of Brush-built open-top bogie cars moves through Dartmouth Square, passing the 1885 cast-iron Farley drinking fountain. The building behind the fountain dates from 1889 and is still occupied by Perry's, its first retail tenant, who preceded the long-lived Broadhead's bread and cake shop, who moved in around 1908. The detail regarding the arrangement of the tram's bogies is interesting. The tram is mounted on Brush Maximum Traction B-type bogies. This means that the tram has two small pony wheels and two large driving wheels on each bogie. Normally the driving wheels would be at the outer end, enabling around 80 per cent of the tram's weight to be carried by the larger diameter wheels. The small pony wheels would be mounted inbound and were used to provide stability when the tram was on a section of curved track or a bend. The South Staffordshire bogie cars were, however, equipped with the maximum traction bogies in the reverse position with the pony wheels leading, apparently to allow sufficient clearance under the platform on tight bends. The result was that these company bogie cars were frequently derailed as there was insufficient weight on the leading pony wheels to keep the tram on what were often sections of worn and poor quality trackwork. (D. R. Harvey Collection)

South Staffordshire 59 *(Top)*

South Staffordshire Tram 59 makes its way along High Street and is about to cross the tracks leading to the left across Dartmouth Square and into Spon Lane as it travels towards the distant Handsworth boundary terminus. SS Tram 59 was built in 1902 for the Wolverhampton District Tramways Company by Brush as part of the WD 14-30 series of tramcars and these were numbered 57–60 in the South Staffordshire fleet after their transfer in about 1915. They were fitted with six framed saloon windows and could be distinguished from the rest of the tram fleet by these distinctive windows and the deep cove panel above the windows. The four trams were always used on the Handsworth boundary to Dudley route. (D. R. Harvey Collection)

512 Class Car *(Opposite below)*

The policeman on point duty at the junction of High Street and the roads leading through Dartmouth Square to the left seems oblivious to the large Humber saloon car bearing down on him. The distant Birmingham Corporation Tramways Department double-deck bogie car is one of the 512 Class built by UEC during late 1913 and early 1914 that still has its open balcony. Work began on the enclosing of the balconies on the seventy-five 512 Class trams after May 1926, a task which took Kyotts Lake Road works some five years. The tram is working on the 75 route from Wednesbury in, therefore, the mid-1920s, and is being followed along High Street by a couple of Sentinel steam lorries. (Commercial Postcard)

Car 545 *(Above)*

Totally-enclosed UEC bogie car 545 passes Dartmouth Square in West Bromwich High Street on 31 March 1939, when working on the 74 route from Dudley to Birmingham. In the background is Marks & Spencers' store and Burton's men's outfitters, each having their own distinctive architectural styles whose presence on the High Street seemed to uplift any shopping area. Dartmouth Square, which was the heart of West Bromwich, was named after the earls of Dartmouth, who as the Legge family moved to Sandwell Hall in 1701. Where the tram stands is the present-day site of the Farley Centre, while the high street is now pedestrianised between Dartmouth Square and St Michael's Street. The only building to survive is Burtons, in its usual 'house style' of 1930s art deco. On the same side of the high street, behind the tram, is the site of the grocery and tea-dealing establishment opened by Joseph Parker in 1834. This was a predecessor of the country's first George Mason grocery chain shop. Car 545 went to Selly Oak depot by June 1939, but was stored after collision damage from December 1940 until May 1946! Even after its return to service, it didn't last long, being finally taken out of service in July 1950. (H. B. Priestley)

Car 619 *(Opposite above)*
Built in early 1921 by Brush of Loughborough, originally with open balconies and sixty-two seats, the fifty trams of the class were mounted on Brush Burnley maximum traction bogies. In 1927 the trams had their balconies enclosed and were re-motored with 63 hp DK30/1L motors over a four-year period. This vastly improved their performance when in service on the West Bromwich services, where speeds of around 40 mph were not uncommon, especially on the last 'turn' back to the depot at Hockley. Car 619 was the second member of the class to be withdrawn, being broken up at Miller Street in March 1950 after an accident. It is standing at Dartmouth Square when working on a football special to The Hawthorns in March 1939 and has the abandonment notices pasted onto the balcony windows. Behind the brand new Hillman Minx car is one of West Bromwich Corporation's Dennis Ace single-deckers. (D. R. Harvey Collection)

South Staffordshire Tram *(Opposite below)*
High Street in West Bromwich was one of the few places in the West Midlands where, when the electric tram system opened, in this case on 19 December 1902, the traction poles were mounted along the centre of the carriageway. Normal span wiring replaced the centre poles at the beginning of 1913. A South Staffordshire tramcar travels along the high street in about 1905 as two young women enthusiastically pedal their bicycles in the opposite direction. (Commercial Postcard)

Car 520 *(Above)*
In High Street, in the centre of West Bromwich's main shopping street, is Car 520. It is approaching Dartmouth Square and is passing the Warwickshire Complete Home Furnishers shop, working on the 77 shortworking from Carter's Green. This UEC-built 70 hp bogie tramcar dated originally from 1914 but had been much rebuilt in the 1920s with enclosed vestibules and platforms. The tram has just reversed at the St Michael's Street terrace of shops just short of New Street, where the wonderfully fronted Sandwell Public House is located. In the distance is the large Kenrick & Jefferson stationery and printing works, dating from 1882 and which was occupied by the company until 1995. (W. A. Camwell)

High Street, West Bromwich

Car 533 *(Top)*

On a rainy day in 1938, a UEC totally enclosed bogie car, equipped with a pair of GEC WT32R 70 hp motors especially for the required high-speed running on the West Bromwich services, travels along the high street towards Birmingham. It is working on the 73 route from Carter's Green. The driver is using the tram's rain-shield; Birmingham tramcars were not fitted with the luxury of windscreen wipers and this usage of the shield by the drivers was the way in which vision was improved in rainy conditions. The tram has just passed the junction with New Street. In the background the tall building belongs to Kenrick & Jefferson, one of the largest printing companies in Britain, making stationery, calendars and greetings cards. In 1937 the West Bromwich Corporation began to evaluate

a number of bus chassis manufacturers' oil-engined buses for evaluation purposes prior to the conversion of the 74 and 75 tram routes on 1 April 1939. The distant double-deck bus is one of these trialled buses. 64 (EA 9001), a Daimler COG6 with a fifty-six-seat Metro-Cammell body, proved to be the successful type and became the precursor of some thirty-five similar buses purchased in 1939 and 1940 for tram replacement purposes. It could always be recognised as it was the only COG6 in the fleet to have the area beneath the front number plate painted blue and not cream. It is working a Football Special from Stone Cross via Tantany to The Hawthorns, and is being passed by a small Dennis Ace with a locally built twenty-seat W. D. Smith body. (D. R. Harvey Collection)

South Staffordshire 15 *(Opposite below)*
The South Staffordshire Tramways (Lessee) Co. opened the first part of its electric tramway, from the Woodman Inn at the Handsworth boundary to Carter's Green, on 10 December 1902. The route was extended over the B&M tracks beyond Burnt Tree to Dudley Station on 30 May 1903. Judging by the crowds standing in High Street at the Dartmouth Square junction, this might be that first day of operation. Standing under the unusual centre pole wiring, replaced in about 1913 by span wires, is Tramcar 15, which was one of the South Staffordshire's large seventy-seat Brush-built bogies dating from 1902. (Commercial Postcard)

Car 548 *(Above)*
Travelling on a 75 service from Wednesbury along High Street, West Bromwich, near to the cross-over at St Michael's Street, is Car 548, a recently totally-enclosed UEC-built bogie car built in early 1914. The car in the foreground is a Standard 14/28 four-door tourer dating from about 1926 which would be about four years old. On the left, with the magnificent lantern over the main door, is the Sandwell Public House located on the corner of New Street. (Commercial Postcard)

South Staffordshire Tramways Co. Ltd *(Top)*

A South Staffordshire steam tram trundles along High Street on a steam tram route that was first authorised in 1881, although it would take until 16 July 1883 before it was opened between Handsworth and Darlaston. This was real pioneering stuff by the South Staffordshire Company! The Victorian engineers rarely did anything by halves and this, the first steam tram service anywhere in the Black Country, was an amazing 4 miles and 3 furlongs long. In addition, there was a second line from Carter's Green via Great Bridge to Dudley that was another 3 miles and 2 furlongs long. The steam tram is travelling away from the distant tower of the Gothic-styled West Bromwich Town Hall, which had been opened in 1875. (D. R. Harvey Collection)

South Staffordshire Steam Tram 12 *(Opposite below)*

Beyer Peacock Steam Tram 12, the last of ten introduced in 1883, stands outside the walled church yard of Christ Church in West Bromwich High Street. The Regency church was consecrated in 1829 and thus was, by ecclesiastical standards, still quite new. These locomotives had vertical boilers and a geared drive from two vertical cylinders which were designed and patented by the Wilkinson Company, who were based in Wigan. Their design was sub-contracted to several locomotive builders, including Beyer Peacock. (D. R. Harvey Collection)

Carters Green

Car 597 *(Above)*

Brush-built bogie Car 597 was to become the very last tram to be broken up at Kyotts Lake Road Works on Thursday 6 August 1953. On Friday 31 March 1939, it rattles across the points in Carters Green as it works towards the stop alongside the Farley Clock. The trams would be replaced by West Bromwich and Birmingham Corporation buses on the following Sunday morning and the notice informing passengers of this change-over have been displayed in the upper saloon balcony window for well over a week. Tram 597 is working on the Dudley-bound 74 service and is being overtaken by a Morris Eight Series II. The tram will take the tracks going to the right, alongside the parked West Bromwich-registered Ford 7W Tudor, and stop outside the Tower Cinema. (H. B. Priestley)

Car 522 *(Top)*

The last day of operation of the West Bromwich routes was 31 May 1939. Car 522 travels over the track junction to take the tram on to the tracks for Dudley. Car 522 has the abandonment notices in the window and as if to add insult to injury, one of Birmingham's replacement buses, 271 (EOG 271), travels towards Carter's Green on a late driver familiarisation duty. This is a Leyland Titan TD6c with an MCCW H28/24R body; this was a chassis type unique to Birmingham and while very smooth with its torque convertor gearbox, it was not very economic on fuel oil. (H. B. Priestley)

South Staffordshire 15 *(Opposite below)*

South Staffordshire Car 15 was built by Brush in 1902 and mounted on Brush maximum traction bogies with the small pony wheels mounted outwards. It had a seating capacity of thirty-four inside and thirty-six outside, which was reached by reverse stairs. It is standing in Carters Green, just short of the elaborate Farley Clock Tower that had been completed in 1897 in time for Queen Victoria's Diamond Jubilee. The tram is working to Dudley and will take the left fork into Dudley Street, alongside the large Methodist chapel, which had been opened in 1876, ironically on the site of the Junction Inn, an old coaching hostelry. Beyond the tram, to the right of the junction, is Old Meeting Street, which led to Hill Top and Wednesbury. (D. R. Harvey Collection)

South Staffordshire 8 and 23 *(Right)*

Standing in Carters Green, just short of the elaborate Farley Clock Tower, are two South Staffordshire open-top tramcars working on the Dudley route. On the right is Bogie Car 23, one of the 1903 Brush-built cars mounted on reversed Brush maximum traction bogies; like the tram next to it, Car 23 has been equipped

with platform screens. These 34½-foot-long tramcars were real giants of their day and had a seating capacity of seventy passengers. The tram on the left, facing West Bromwich and Handsworth, is an unidentified open-top four-wheeler. The Farley Clock Tower had been completed in 1897 and is inscribed: 'This tower was erected in recognition of the public services of Alderman Reuben Farley JP.' On three sides there are relief panels of the Town Hall, Oak House and Reuben Farley, the latter being clearly visible. The clock tower was Grade II Listed in 1987. Farley was involved with a number of prominent Black Country businesses including canal carriers, the chairman of boilermakers and boat builders Edwin Danks, director of the Sandwell Park Colliery and chairman of Hamstead Colliery. He served as mayor five times but was determined to build a permanent legacy for West Bromwich. Among the many benefits Farley brought to West Bromwich, the most prominent is Dartmouth Park, which he worked so hard to establish. The Tudor-built Oak House, which he had bought with the intention of it becoming his home, was donated to the town as a working museum. He encouraged the development of the town's gas supplies and ensured that water supplies and sewerage beds were built. Additionally, he pushed through legislation to build libraries, swimming baths, hospitals, colleges and schools. He died in 1899 aged seventy-three. (D. R. Harvey Collection)

CLOCK TOWER, CARTERS GREEN.

South Staffordshire 31 *(Opposite above)*
Standing at the junction of Dudley Street and Old Meeting Street was the old Methodist chapel, which was opened in May 1876 and closed in 1949. This had been built on the site of the old Junction Inn. The South Staffordshire Co. had opened the line to the White Horse at Wednesbury on 8 October 1903. In approximately 1914, about to turn from Old Meeting Street into Carter's Green, is a South Staffordshire Black Country Through Car. Car 31 was an open-balcony tramcar with open vestibules, which left the motorman open to the elements. This Brush-bodied tram, mounted on Brush-built Lycett & Conaty Radial trucks, entered service in 1904 and was first owned by B&M. It was transferred to SS in 1907 and some three years later was fitted with a top-cover especially to operate the Black Country Through Car service, which opened on 9 October 1912. By 1914 the trams ran every sixteen minutes, taking sixty-four minutes from Birmingham to Darlaston. To travel from Colmore Row to the Handsworth boundary cost 2*d* and, after re-booking at The Hawthorns, cost another 4½*d* to Darlaston. (Commercial Postcard)

Car 561 *(Opposite below)*
Not long after Birmingham Corporation Tramways took over the operation of the tram routes through West Bromwich, previously operated by the South Staffordshire (Lessee) Company, on 1 April 1924, Car 561 approaches the queues of waiting passengers at the tram stop beneath the Farley Clock in Carter's Green. It has already left the high street tracks and is turning into Old Meeting Street as it prepares to travel towards Wednesbury on the 75 route. Behind the clock is the 1876 Methodist church, which dominated the apex of this important junction. Car 561, built in 1914 by UEC, is still in its original condition with open balconies. (Commercial Postcard)

Cars 517 and 519 *(Top)*
A point of transition! Standing at the Farley Clock Tower in Carter's Green in the summer of 1927, when working on the 75 route, are two of the 512 Class of bogie trams, both dating from October 1913. On the left, approaching the stop for Wednesbury, is Car 517, whose balconies were enclosed during April 1927, whereas on the right is the still open balconied Car 519, which was not dealt with until December 1928. (Commercial Postcard)

CARTERS GREEN, WEST BROMWICH.

Car 614 *(Opposite above)*

A totally enclosed Birmingham Corporation Brush-bodied bogie car stands at the tram stop in Carter's Green with Old Meeting Street behind it to the right. To the left of the Farley Clock and the Methodist chapel is Dudley Street. In about 1930, Tram 614, dating from the end of 1920, is travelling towards West Bromwich on the 75 service. Beneath the clock is the substantial passenger shelter, which had been joined fairly recently by a K3 concrete telephone box. These distinctive cast iron structures had been designed by Sir Giles Gilbert Scott in 1929, with about 12,000 appearing over the country. (Commercial Postcard)

South Staffordshire 18 *(Opposite below)*

In the early years of electric tram operation by the South Staffordshire (Lessee), Car 18 has arrived at the Farley Clock in Carter's Green from Wednesbury. The reddish-brown liveried bogie tram was constructed by Brush in 1903 and had a capacity of thirty-six outside and thirty-four in the lower saloon. They had reversed Brush B-type maximum traction bogies and Brush 1002B 33 hp motors and were initially well equipped for the long route between Handsworth and Darlaston. Unfortunately, the often poor company maintenance resulted in an increasingly rapid deterioration of both their reliability and the state of their bodywork, which meant that withdrawals began during the First World War. (Commercial Postcard)

Car 516 *(Top)*

In about 1927, UEC-bodied Car 516, still with open balconies, leaves the Farley Clock in Carter's Green on its way to Birmingham on the 75 service from Wednesbury. Trams 512–533 and 534 were at Rosebery Street depot from new and were originally fitted with a pair of DK 19A3 40 hp motors. They were transferred to Hockley depot and were almost immediately re-motored with GEC WT32R 70 hp motors for the long, fast parts of the route. Speeds of up to 40 mph were not unheard of, especially on the sections across the Sandwell Valley, from Carter's Green to Great Bridge and from Hill Top to Wednesbury. (Commercial Postcard)

Car 551 *(Top)*

A very smart-looking car 551 approaches the Farley Clock, Carter's Green, when working
on the 74 route to Dudley in 1938. This was one of ten of the 512 Class equipped with a new
design of top cover which had eight windows per side as opposed to the more normal four.
The idea was that it enabled each row of seats to have its own opening window, but it did
give the body a somewhat fussy appearance. Car 551 was the last tram from Colmore Row
to Wednesbury on the 75 route on the evening of 1 April 1939. It ran only as far as Carter's

Green on the return journey, whereupon all its passengers were put on the old four-wheeler Car 128, which would be withdrawn for scrap after its return to Hockley as the last tram into the depot. Thus spared the vandalism expected on the last tram, Car 551 went outwards to Dudley and was immediately driven to its new home at Selly Oak depot, unusually by way of Oldbury and West Smethwick, where bogie cars were a rarity. (R. Wilson)

Cars 517, 520 and 549 *(Opposite below)*
The Farley Clock in Carter's Green not only marked the end of the 'Golden Mile' of West Bromwich High Street, but also the point at which the routes to Dudley diverged. To the right, cars 517 and 520 are on the 75 route, the former inbound and 520 travelling towards Wednesbury. Of the two cars on the track to the left of the clock, only the second tram, Brush-bodied Car 608 of 1920, is working into Birmingham from Dudley on the 74 route. UEC-built Tramcar 548, on the 73 route, has turned after reversing at the cross-over at the clock tower. This 1938 scene shows the 1876 Methodist church in the background. This survived until 1970 when, after several years as a warehouse, it was demolished because of the future road widening that has now left the clock as an isolated traffic island. (W. A. Camwell)

Car 558, 551 and 632 *(Above)*
Tramcar operation continued normally despite the impending abandonment on 1 April 1939, with bus stops being put into place the previous week being about the only clues to the change-over. But looking carefully, Car 632 has a number of posters in both saloons, suggesting that these are the public pronouncement of information about the replacement bus services. Car 558, working on a Dudley-bound 74 service, approaches the eight-windowed, top-decked Car 551, waiting at the tram shelters at Carter's Green as it waits to continue its journey into West Bromwich. On the right is Car 632, a Brush-bodied tram dating from 1920, which is turning back to West Bromwich having worked on the 73 short working to Carter's Green. (Ribble Enthusiasts Club)

Cars 562 and 600 *(Top)*

Looking from the Old Meeting Street side of the Farley Clock in 1939 are two tramcars, working on each of the routes that operated through West Bromwich. On the right is UEC Bogie Car 562 of 1914, which is working on the 75 route to Wednesbury. On the far side of the clock tower is Brush-bodied Bogie Tram 600, coming into West Bromwich on an inbound 74 service from Dudley. The tram is in Dudley Street not far from the present day Metro stop at Guns' village. Both trams were delivered with open balconies but were enclosed in the late 1920s, to virtually the same design, though on the rebuilt 512 Class of trams the end balcony window below the route number box was square, whereas on the later 587 Class it was rectangular and slightly larger. To the left of Car 600 and just out of shot is the art deco designed Tower Cinema. (R. T. Wilson)

South Staffordshire Tram *(Above)*

The mid-nineteenth century development of Carter's Green had been extensively built up by the 1880s, although development around the main road to Shrewsbury had begun in

stagecoach days, with some buildings dating from the 1820s. A South Staffordshire bogie car has left Carter's Green going towards West Bromwich and is about opposite John Street. The electric trams reached Carter's Green on 19 December 1902. The next sections of the route were opened in small sections, either delayed by local leasing disagreements or by the slow construction of the tramway infrastructure. The section to Great Bridge, on the right of the Farley Clock, was opened very quickly on 24 January 1903 and the Hill Top section opened just twenty-six days later on 19 February. On 19 April the route was extended to Holloway Bank, Wednesbury, while the Great Bridge branch was extended to Dudley using B&M tracks on 30 May 1903. (Commercial Postcard)

Car 144 (Above)

The short working 73 tram route to Carter's Green terminated alongside the famous four-faced Farley Clock. In 1937, Car 144 stands next to one of the newly erected Belisha Beacons, introduced in 1934 by the Transport Minister, the Right Hon. Leslie Hore-Belisha (1803–1957), as one of the many attempts in the 1930s to reduce the number of pedestrian fatalities and injuries in towns and cities. Car 144 entered service in late 1906 as one of the 150 Radial trucked trams built for Birmingham Corporation. The Mountain & Gibson Radial trucks proved to be unsatisfactory and all were replaced, with Car 144 getting Brush-built Peckham P35 trucks during the 1920s. In 1938, Hockley depot's tram allocation of seventy-seven trams contained twenty-six of these small 71 Class trams, which were due for early withdrawal and were used usually on short working and peak hour services. The tram was re-motored in 1934 with a DK13A 40 hp motor, and when it was withdrawn in September 1939 it was stored in Rosebery Street depot. Car 144 became one of twenty-two of the 71 Class retained in reserve throughout the Second World War. (R. T. Wilson)

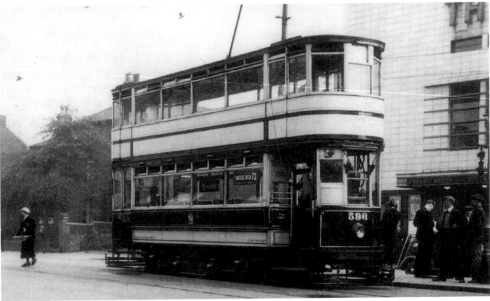

Car 600 *(Top)*

Car 600, ordered in 1920, was one of the first trams ordered after the First World War. It was fitted with an eight-windowed top deck in September 1930. Facing West Bromwich, Car 600 is loading up with passengers while it waits at the tram shelters in Carter's Green when working on the 74 service. Just visible next to the phone box is the square, brick-built Farley Clock, which had been erected in 1897 to recognise the philanthropic achievements of the five-time Mayor of West Bromwich Reuben Farley (1826–1899). Behind the tram in the distance is the row of three-storied early nineteenth-century premises. (D. R. Harvey Collection)

Car 596 *(Opposite below)*

At Carter's Green the two tram routes diverged, with the 74 route forking slightly to the left through Great Bridge to Dudley, while the 75 route went to the right of the Farley Clock Tower via Hill Top to Wednesbury. Car 596, trolley-pole turned for the return run to Birmingham and working on the short working 73 service, stands outside the Tower Cinema at the Carter's Green terminus on 9 August 1938. The Tower is showing as its main feature film *The Buccaneer*, starring Fredric March and Akim Tamiroff. The Tower Cinema opened on 9 December 1935 with the Alfred Hitchcock classic version of John Buchan thriller novel *The Thirty-Nine Steps*. It starred Robert Donat and Madeleine Carroll. It was appropriate that this film should have been shown as the cinema's first feature as although of French-Irish parents, Madeleine Carroll was born in West Bromwich in 1906. The cinema, with its splendid art deco front, closed in 1968 and, after a period as a bingo hall, was demolished in the 1980s. Car 596 survived until December 1952, when it was withdrawn with flatted wheels and split pinions. (W. A. Camwell)

Car 516 *(Above)*

This unique photograph from the balcony of a tramcar looks into Dudley Street, where Car 516 waits at the tram shelters on an inbound 74 service. It is 31 May 1939 and the following day would see buses operating on the 74 and 75 services. There would still be a lot of tramcar activity after the closure but this would consist of trams being transferred from Hockley to other depots in Birmingham. The tram tracks at Carter's Green would be soon either ripped up or tarmaced over and the complex junction in the foreground would soon become just a memory. (H. B. Priestley)

To Dudley

Car 545

After leaving Carter's Green, the 74 route passed through Swan Village before reaching the Market Place at Great Bridge. Great Bridge developed in the 1780s when the Ryder's Green branch of the Wednesbury–Birmingham canal was opened. The district had a further boost to its prosperity when the London & North Western Railway developed two interchange points with the canal at the Great Bridge Basin in the mid-nineteenth century. These were some of the last canal/railway interchange points to remain, falling into disuse in the early 1960s. The short-working to Great Bridge was numbered 76, but only one or two peak journeys and a couple after the last Dudley service at night were scheduled. UEC Tramcar 545 stands outside Lloyds Bank in the centre of Great Bridge when working on a 74 service tram on 9 August 1938. (W. A. Camwell)

Car 609

UEC-bodied Tramcar 609 squeezes through the low bridge on its way from Dudley on 7 September 1938 when working on the 74 route. Trams were subject to a 4 mph speed limit here because of the point work leading into the single-line section under both the aqueduct and the railway bridge, and because of the slewed overhead which took the trolley-pole wide of the tramcar to the western side of the arched bridges. Only bogie top-covered trams operated by BCT were allowed through the bridges at Dudley Port and these carried a rectangular plate on the signal lamp rails, with the inscription: 'LOW BRIDGE CAR: SELLY OAK, ASTON, and DUDLEY PORT', which were the three low bridges on the Birmingham system. (W. A. Camwell)

Car 617 *(Opposite above)*
Dudley Port was the name of the road as well as the district, and seen here climbing up Dudley Port towards Burnt Tree on the 74 route is Brush-built Bogie Car 617. It is Thursday 14 April 1938 and the tram, which is nearly full, has just overtaken a large Austin Twenty Saloon motorcar parked near to the Waggon & Horses, an Atkinson public house that occupied No. 71 Dudley Port. UEC-bodied Car 617 had been allocated to Hockley depot for most of its service life since it entered service in 1920. (H. B. Priestley)

Car 634 *(Opposite below)*
At Burnt Tree on Wednesday 6 September 1938, Brush-bodied Bogie Car 634, dating from early 1921, travels across New Birmingham Road on the 74 route. On the right is one of the 71 Class cars coming out of Tividale Road, working on the 87 service. The cyclist on the right is using a bike with drop handlebars, which were still a rarity before the war, except with racing cycles. The two routes and the New Birmingham Road made a grassy triangle, long since subsumed by the enlargement of this important road junction with traffic lights and motorway-width carriageways. (W. A. Camwell)

Cars 532 and 154 *(Above)*
The junction between Dudley Road and Tividale Road at Burnt Tree Crossing, where the still fairly recently built New Birmingham Road avoided Dudley town centre, was where the 'main line' from West Bromwich met 'The Track' from Oldbury. In about 1938, on the right of the junction coming from Tividale Road, is UEC-bodied open-balcony former radial truck four-wheeler Car 154. The tram is working on the 87 route. On the left is UEC-bodied Bogie Tramcar 532, whose driver has extended the vestibule sun visor on this sunny day. It is operating on the 74 service from West Bromwich. (W. A. Camwell)

Car 521 *(Opposite above)*

Car 521 is about to join the former B&M tracks that brought the 87 route from Oldbury. Car 521 is a UEC-bodied bogie totally enclosed tramcar working on the 74 service during the last few weeks of the route, on a miserable day in March 1939. It is travelling from West Bromwich, Great Bridge and Dudley Port to Burnt Tree, where they crossed the Birmingham New Road. This had been opened by HRH the Prince of Wales on 2 November 1927. From this Burnt Tree junction to the terminus at the bottom of Castle Hill, from 30 March 1903, the original South Staffordshire cars were able to run over B&M-owned track. (R. T. Coxon)

Car 93 *(Opposite below)*

In 1938 Car 93 is in Birmingham Road, Burnt Tree, when working on the 87 route from Oldbury on its way into Dudley. This UEC-bodied former Radial-truck car of 1906 was one of the trams allocated to Rosebery Street depot at the time of the mass upheaval of tramcar allocations, when all the Soho Road routes and those to West Bromwich and beyond were abandoned and Hockley depot was closed on 1 April 1939. Car 93 would not survive this – it was deemed to be one of thirty-three 71 Class tramcars in poor condition and was taken out of service on 6 April 1939. A Singer Bantam two-door saloon car is parked outside the houses on the left, a site which is now occupied by a huge Tesco superstore. (J. S. Webb)

South Staffordshire Steam Tram 9 *(Top)*

Standing at the Dudley Station terminus in Birmingham Road is Beyer Peacock steam locomotive 9, built in 1883 for the South Staffordshire Tramway Company as one of the ten numbered 3–12. It is working on the Handsworth to Dudley route and is pulling trailer 17. The fifty-two-seat, plate-framed bogie trailer car had been built by Falcon of Loughborough in late 1883. The steam route reached Dudley on 12 October 1885, from Great Bridge, and lasted until its conversion to electric traction on 30 May 1903. (H. Whitcombe Collection)

South Staffordshire Car 23 *(Opposite above)*
An almost new, large South Staffordshire maximum traction bogie, Car 23, built by Brush in early 1903 with a capacity of seventy passengers, waits at the bottom of Castle Hill in about 1910. The tram is working on the Dudley to Handsworth service and is standing in front of the original Victorian Station Hotel, which was demolished in 1936 and replaced by the building which thrives today. On the right is the forested Castle Hill, which has on it Dudley's famous Norman castle, dating from around 1071. Car 23 is standing on the junction leading into Tipton Road, which was used by South Staffordshire Tramways (Lessee) Company for the Princes End and Wednesbury route as well as gaining access to their depot opposite Dudley Town Railway Station. These trams led with their bogie pony wheels, which resulted in the trams being prone to derailment on poor track. (D. R. Harvey Collection)

Car 553 *(Opposite below)*
In 1936, UEC-bodied bogie Tram 553 stands at the Dudley terminus of the 74 route. The wall next to the tram is the parapet of the railway bridge over the line for trains going to either Stourbridge or Halesowen, while behind the tram is the Station Hotel. In pre-war days Dudley had two railway stations adjoining each other, just across the road from the hotel. Originally built in 1910, The Station Hotel was demolished in 1936 and replaced by a larger hotel. This became popular with theatrical artists playing the Hippodrome Theatre, across the other side of Castle Hill. (D. R. Harvey Collection)

Car 154 *(Top)*
On 23 August 1937, Car 154 stands on the railway bridge at the Dudley terminus of the 87 route. A large Austin-20 car being used as a taxi for passengers leaving the railway station waits at the bottom of Castle Hill, in the shadow of the Dudley Hippodrome Theatre. It was built on the site of the Dudley Opera House, which had burnt down in 1936 and was still under construction in the summer of 1937. A 1,700-seat venue, the art deco-styled Hippodrome Theatre was one of the largest variety venues in the West Midlands and survived until 1964; it is still extant, awaiting possible restoration. Next door to it is the also then-unfinished Plaza Cinema. Just short of the trees on Castle Hill is the entrance to Dudley Zoo, which was opened on 18 May 1937. (W. A. Camwell)

Car 607 and 843 *(Top)*

The LRTA organised a tour of the Birmingham tram system using Birmingham's newest, and what turned out to be last, tramcar, 843. On Sunday 23 October 1938, Car 843 stands at the by now long-truncated trackwork at the bottom of Castle Hill at the junction with Trindle Road. In the distance, a Midland Red SOS FEDD waits to leave the stop outside the Station Hotel before heading off to Brierley Hill. Parked on the railway bridge at the impressive tram stop notice is Brush-bodied Car 607, which is working on the 74 route and has already had its trolley pole turned for the return journey back to West Bromwich and Birmingham. (L. W. Perkins)

Car 625 *(Opposite below)*

The end of the 9-mile journey to Dudley was just beyond Midland Red's garage, which is the building to the extreme left of the photograph and which had opened on 2 August 1929. Car 625, a Brush-built bogie car, waits at the terminus just beyond Midland Red's Dudley garage, ready to return to Birmingham on the 74 service on 23 October 1938. This was the same day as the LRTA trip of the Birmingham tram system with lightweight Brush-built tram 843. Immaculately turned out, the eighteen-year-old tram still retains the old 'Birmingham Corporation Tramways and Omnibus Dept' legal lettering on its rocker panel, showing that it had not been repainted since the title was changed in November 1937. In the late 1930s it was quite common for the trams to have posters advertising local events on their fenders, in this case the Birmingham University Hospital Carnival Fair. (A. N. H. Glover)

165, 523, 518 *(Above)*

Parked on the railway bridge on Birmingham Road on 9 August 1938 are BCT trams 165 and 523. Just visible to the right of the distant Car 518 is Midland Red's Dudley garage with an SOS SLR coach. The four-wheeled 165 was fitted with a fifty-two-seater open-balconied body built by UEC and delivered in late 1906. Originally equipped with a Mountain & Gibson 8-foot 6-inch-long radial truck, Car 165 was fitted with Brush Peckham P35 trucks in the mid-1920s. The contrast between these elderly trams whose last operational duties involved their use on the Oldbury route is quite marked when compared with the totally-enclosed tram behind it operating on the 74 service. Car 523, a UEC-bodied bogie car of 1913, has already had its trolley pole turned as a man wearing a gabardine mackintosh rushes to get onto the tram. The irony, in terms of the routes at least, was that the more modern trams were working on the route which would be abandoned first, while the older tram's route would survive for six months. Car 165 survived until 30 September 1939 and was broken up at West Smethwick depot yard during the following April, whereas the bogie tram was withdrawn in June 1951 from Selly Oak depot after its bodywork was found defective. (W. A. Camwell)

Car 80 *(Top)*

Having turned the trolley pole around, the conductor gets onto the platform of open-balconied, four-wheel Car 80 before preparing to set off. It is 21 May 1939 and the tram is working on the 87 service to Birmingham via Tividale, Oldbury, Smethwick and Cape Hill, though the destination blind only shows the outer termini in true BCT fashion. Parked outside the Midland Red garage is an MCCW-bodied SOS FEDD, dating from

1936, which is working on a 246 service to Stourbridge by way of Harts Hill, Brierley Hill and Amblecote. That route was originally opened by the Dudley & Stourbridge Tramway on 7 December 1900 and finally closed in two stages in December 1925 and April the following year. (J. C. Gillham)

Car 535 *(Opposite below)*
The last tramcar to leave Dudley via West Bromwich was UEC-bodied totally-enclosed bogie Car 535, which ran back as far as Carters Green to be replaced by the ex-Radial four-wheel Car 128. Car 535 was at Moseley Road depot by the following Saturday. The enthusiasts lean out of the top deck to be recorded for posterity as the tram stands on the railway bridge at the bottom of Castle Hill for the last time. (D. R. Harvey Collection)

To Wednesbury

South Staffordshire 42 *(Above)*
On the Wednesbury service in South Staffordshire days, Car 42 passes Hill Top Primary School with its pair of cupola bell-towers guarding the site, at the junction with Coles Lane. These Edwardian school buildings were opened in 1911 as a council school with four departments: senior boys, senior girls, junior mixed, and infants. It was finally demolished in 1994. The tram is travelling towards the steep descent of Holloway Bank as it goes on to the terminus at the White Horse Hotel in Bridge Street, Wednesbury. Almost certainly this is a Black Country Through Car which will terminate in Bilston. Car 42 was built as an open-top in 1904 by Brush for Birmingham & Midland Company. Known as the 'Aston' type, this was one of a number of trams transferred to the South Staffs operation in 1912, in time for the introduction of the new Black Country Through Car service. (D. R. Harvey Collection)

South Staffordshire Steam Tram *(Top)*
Accompanied by a marching brass band, with the bass drum almost as big as the drummer, an almost new Wilkinson-Patent, Beyer Peacock-built vertical-boilered steam tram hauls a Falcon-built double-deck trailer through Hill Top. The steam tram was inaugurating the new service between Handsworth via West Bromwich and Wednesbury to Darlaston on 16 July 1883. According to the local press, the trams 'were equipped with cushioned seats inside, while those who travel outside will be protected by an awning either from the sun or the inclemency of the weather'. The trailer is carrying the almost obligatory advertisement for the West Bromwich-produced Hudson's Soap. (D. R. Harvey Collection)

Car 565 *(Opposite below)*

Car 565 is on Holloway Bank, on the 75 route, on the last day of tram operation to Wednesbury on 31 March 1939. The steep 's' bend into the Tame Valley from Hill Top to Wednesbury dated from the nineteenth century and eased the climb out of the valley for road traffic at a time when Wednesbury had been one of the cornerstones of the Industrial Revolution in the Black Country. From being one of the world's most important iron-producing centres in the mid-eighteenth century, Wednesbury was linked by canal to Birmingham as early as 1769, by the end of the nineteenth century the town had specialised in the making of steel tubes. The cobbled main road and the slightly run-down nature of the houses on Holloway Bank reflect an air of previous prosperity that had been badly hit since the First World War. The tram remained in service until July 1953. (R. T. Wilson)

Car 592 *(Above)*

On Holloway Bank, Hill Top, on Friday 31 March 1939, Brush-built Car 592 is going towards the Wednesbury terminus about three-quarters of a mile away at the White Horse Hotel. The tram has the route abandonment notice in the balcony window. This section of the 75 route had some notoriously poor-quality track and after a threat was made by Birmingham to withdraw the service, the track was renewed in the mid-1930s, albeit reluctantly, by West Bromwich Corporation, which was responsible for its upkeep. Latterly this allowed for some spirited performances on the sharp descent into Wednesbury and just as in the South Staffordshire steam tram days, complaints were received, orders issued and the drivers continued as before once the dust had settled. The steep 'S' bend into the Tame Valley had originally been developed for horse-drawn wagons to ease the climb up to Hill Top. This occurred during the mid-eighteenth century, when Wednesbury was one of the world's largest producers of iron and subsequently steel tubes. By the 1930s the Depression had badly hit the town, and, with unemployment reaching over 30 per cent, the area was becoming extremely run down. Struggling up the steep hill is a horse and cart which at just at the crucial moment has got into the photograph. (R. T. Wilson)

South Staffordshire Tramways Co. Ltd, Wilkinson Type *(Top)*

Engine No. 11, built by Beyer Peacock in 1883 with a vertical boiler built to the Wilkinson Patents and a six-bay construction Falcon-built trailer car, stands at the White Horse public house, Wednesbury, when working on the Darlaston route from Handsworth and West Bromwich. This is between October 1903, when the South Staffordshire electric trams reached the White Horse Hotel, and 15 June 1904, when the Wednesbury to Darlaston steam tram service was finally closed. One of the new open-top, double-deck electric bogie cars is just visible behind the steam tram trailer. (D. R. Harvey Collection)

South Staffordshire 40-55 Class *(Above)*

Standing in front of the Georgian Lloyds Bank building at the junction of Holyhead Road and Lower High Street, Wednesbury, is one of the original South Staffordshire electric tramcars from the 40-55 Class of open-top forty-seaters. These pioneering little

double-deck tramcars opened both this, the Wednesbury to Bloxwich route, and the Darlaston to Mellish Road service on 1 January 1893. The historical significance of this was that it was only the second system in Britain to use the overhead trolley method of current collection and these sixteen trams operated some 7½ miles on these two routes. Towering over the tram is the tower and spire of St John's church, which was built in 1846 and demolished in July 1985. (Commercial Postcard)

Car 613 *(Above)*
The terminus at the White Horse Hotel in Bridge Street, Wednesbury, was the only place in the Black Country where three tramway operators met, although originally it was just two services, both operated by the South Staffordshire (Lessee) Company. This was where the last company trams finally operated in the Black Country on the evening of Tuesday 30 September 1930, but even the route taken over by Walsall Corporation only lasted until 4 March 1931, when it was replaced by the Walsall Corporation 37 route. On the left is an unidentified South Staffordshire car at the terminus of the company service to Darlaston. The tram tracks in the foreground swinging to the left into Holyhead Road were originally used for the SS Black Country Through Car Service. This most useful route linked Birmingham to Bilston and was opened on 9 October 1912. Although offered to Birmingham to operate, after reaching Darlaston with a bogie car the link was severed here opposite the White Horse Hotel on 1 April 1924. The explanation given at the time was that the side running overhead beyond Wednesbury was not suitable for Birmingham's trams, though the state of the worn tram tracks was probably the real reason. BCT Brush totally enclosed bogie tramcar 613, dating from 1921, stands at the awkwardly placed terminus of the 75 route from Colmore Row in Birmingham. On the right is one of Walsall Corporation's 40-49 Class. Built in 1919, this vestibuled, open-balconied Brush-bodied 40 hp four-wheeler was only two years older than the Birmingham bogie car, but looks much older. It only ran for fourteen years before the system closed on 30 September 1933. (Commercial Postcard)

Car 598 (Opposite above)
After the Walsall Corporation tram service to The Bridge was abandoned on 5 March 1931, the junction at Holyhead Road, Lower High Street and Bridge Street was left to the devices of the 75 route trams operated by BCT. In 1938, Brush-bodied Car 598 stands at the Lower High Street terminus. On the right is St John's church, built in 1846, with its impressive Gothic spire, described by Nikolaus Pevsner as 'odd in outline'. The church was notable for having contrasting light and dark stonework. Behind the tram is Lloyds Bank while on the left, standing on the railway bridge over the old South Staffordshire line, is a Morris Eight car dating from 1936. (R. T. Wilson)

Car 603 (Opposite below)
Although the trams stopped in Bridge Street opposite the White Horse Hotel, in reality the terminus was in the middle of High Street where it met Holyhead Road. Here there was a substantial passenger shelter and although technically this was an example of kerbside loading, in reality passengers had to cross at least one main road in order to either gain access to, or leave, their tramcar. Car 603 stands at the shelter, just feet short of the stub terminus which once connected to the Walsall Corporation route into the centre of that town. (J. S. Webb)

Car 514 (Above)
On Saturday 25 March 1939, only one week before the abandonment of the tram service, UEC-bodied tramcar 514, built in 1913, stands at the White Horse Hotel in Wednesbury waiting to return to the city on the 75 route. The immaculately presented tram, one of the UEC-bodied, re-motored high-speed cars, was already twenty-six years old. It is in company with Walsall Corporation's Dennis Lance II bus 202 (FDH 863), with a Park Royal H28/26R body, which was barely six months old and about to return to Walsall via Darlaston on the 37 route. The tram would outlive the nearly new bus by some seventeen months, as it was not withdrawn from service until Friday 4 July 1952, when the Bristol Road routes were closed. (A. N. H. Glover)

Birmingham & Midland Tramways

Birmingham and Midland Tramways Ltd

Birmingham District Power and Traction Co. Ltd (From 13 August 1912) 12.87 miles operated, of which 8.15 owned.

Opened 3 November 1903 and worked by SS until late 1904, closed 17 November 1929.

Birmingham Corporation worked the 'main line' from 1 April 1928 until 30 September 1939.

Livery Munich lake and cream, later Corinthian Green and cream.

The dearth of previously unpublished photographs is purely a reflection on the early closure of these company services.

Bromford Lane and Spon Lane

Crowther Horse Tram 23 *(Opposite below)*

The two original horse trams, numbered 23 and 24, were leased to B. Crowther, a local undertaker, in 1893 by the Birmingham & Midland Tramway Company. These were two Metropolitan Carriage & Wagon Co. sixteen-seaters. Mr Crowther took over from the Birmingham & Midland steam trams, operated on the Spon Lane and Bromford Lane routes somewhat unsuccessfully since 1885 on 20 May 1893, and had ten horses at his disposal. The routes operated from just after 9 a.m. until after 11 p.m. with a thirty-minute headway on the Spon Lane service and a service every forty-five minutes on Bromford Lane. The horse trams were eventually replaced by single-decker electric trams operated by B&M on 3 November 1903. (D. R. Harvey Collection)

Crowther Horse Tram *(Above)*

Standing at the Dartmouth Square terminus of the Spon Lane route is one of the second pair of horse trams bought new by Mr Crowther in about 1896. The five-windowed trams both had a monitor roof and carried the legend 'B. Crowther for Funerals' on one rocker panel and 'B. Crowther for Weddings' on the other one. This is the 'funeral' side! Crowther's stables were in Paradise Street, where his funeral director's premises were located. The yard was linked to both Spon Lane and Bromford Lane by tracks which led directly into his yard at the Bromford Lane end of Paradise Street. (D. R. Harvey Collection)

B&M 53-60 *(Top)*

Eight single-deck closed-combination trams with five side windows, three compartments and a monitor roof were built at the CBT Company's Kyott's Lake Road Works for the Birmingham & Midland Tramways Company Limited in 1904. The tramcars were ordered in mid-October and were delivered at the end of the year. They were described as being for the Rowley Regis service but were soon employed on both the Bromford Lane and Spon Lane routes, which had to be operated by single-deckers because of low bridges and weight restrictions. An unidentified member of the class travels along Bromford Road as it approaches the then Oldbury & Bromford Lane Station on the Stour Valley Line. Originally opened as 'Oldbury' in 1852, it is now known as Sandwell and Dudley. These trams were initially mounted on 8-foot 6-inch wheelbase Lycett & Conaty Radial trucks, built by Brush, as well as having Conaty track brakes but by February 1906 they had been removed, leaving the trams to soldier on with only wheel and rheostatic brakes. (D. R. Harvey Collection)

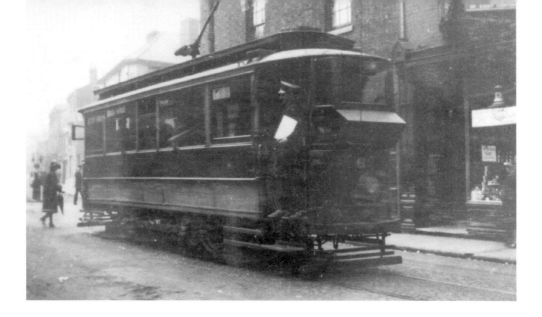

Car 51 *(Opposite below)*

The Spon Lane route was operated using single-deck cars by B&M although there was not a low bridge on this service; but as the Bromford Lane route was restricted by the L&NW railway bridge at Oldbury, the two 'Lanes' services were operated by single-deck trams allocated to Tividale depot. 'Lye'-type single-decker tram 51 has been parked on the newly rebuilt railway bridge in Spon Lane in 1927 along with a steam roller, a steam-traction engine with heavy-duty crane and a steam lorry. This four-bay bodied, totally enclosed single-deck tramcar had been built at Tividale Works in 1915 for the Dudley and Stourbridge section, but when these tram routes were replaced the four Lye types were moved to see out the remaining time on the West Bromwich Lanes services. The track in Spon Lane was by this time extremely bad but the section over the bridge had to be replaced with the new bridge despite West Bromwich Corporation's intention to replace the B&M trams with their own motor buses as soon as was practicable under the West Bromwich Corporation Act of 1927. An agreement was signed between the company and the Corporation on 15 November 1929 and with almost indecent haste the tramway was abandoned two days later. (D. R. Harvey Collection)

Car 62 *(Above)*

Facing the high street in West Bromwich is B&M single-deck tram 62. This closed combination tram was built at Kyotts Lake Road for the B&M in 1904 on Lycett & Conaty 8-foot 6-inch trucks but these were replaced in 1911 with a Brush Flexible 8-foot-long truck. This tram went to the Dudley & Stourbridge Company in 1911 when it lost its original B&M fleet number, 56, and became D&S 62, a number it retained when it was returned in 1925 to its original company. After the end of the First World War, 62 was re-motored with a pair of BTH GE58 37 hp motors. It is standing at the top of Spon Lane, having just arrived from Spon Croft, Oldbury. The gable wall of the Bull's Head is just visible above the tram. The tram conductor holds his waybill under his arm on one of the last days of operation of the route in November 1929. (D. R. Harvey Collection)

Car 1 *(Top)*

Car 1 is working in Spon Lane in the last few weeks of the route's operation in 1929, when the state of the track was noticeably bad. Spon Lane was one of West Bromwich's principal areas of heavy industry, with numerous glassworks and foundries in the vicinity. As a result, Spon Lane became well-known for the number of public houses along its length that were there to slake the thirst of the foundry and furnace men. At one time Spon Lane had over twenty pubs along its one-mile length! The prototype Tividale-style single-decker, Car 1, dated from February 1915 and was one of four built to replace the ageing original single-deckers. These four Dudley & Stourbridge trams were built as low-height saloons with a maximum height of 10 feet 5 inches to the trolley

plank in order to clear the railway bridge at Stourbridge Town Station when used on the Lye service. Although 33 feet long, they were only able to seat thirty-two passengers on the two longitudinal wooden bench seats in the saloon, although this number would double with standing passengers in peak periods. (D. R. Harvey Collection)

Car 2 *(Opposite below)*
Waiting at the Spon Lane terminus at Dartmouth Square is Car 2, a Tividale Lye tram which also dated from February 1915 and was built for the Dudley & Stourbridge section's Lye route. These trams were the first single-decker to have totally enclosed vestibules and roller blind destination blinds and had only the four very large saloon windows. The two Lanes services by this time were operated from the Dudley & Stourbridge depot and main workshops in Tividale rather than from the more obvious West Smethwick depot. The tram is standing alongside the Dartmouth Hotel. The reason for the tram crew posing for posterity is that this is 17 November 1929, which was the last day of tram operation by the Birmingham & Midland Tramways in West Bromwich. (D. R. Harvey Collection)

Car 62 *(Above)*
Standing at the top of Spon Lane, with Dartmouth Square lost in the wet beyond the tram, is Car 62 again. It is waiting to depart for Spon Croft, Oldbury, on the last day of tramcar operation of the route on 15 November 1929. Two days later, West Bromwich Corporation single-deck buses would be operating both the Spon Lane and Bromford Lane routes as Birmingham Corporation Tramways declined to take on either of these routes on the grounds of the low bridge at the then Oldbury Station, which would have necessitated the use of single-deck trams which they did not possess, low revenue except in the peak periods, the poor condition of the trackwork on both routes and virtually any other excuse not to work the routes. Facing the high street in West Bromwich is B&M single-deck closed combination tram 62, which dated from 1904. It has a Brush Flexible 8-foot-long truck and a pair of BTH GE58 37 hp motors, which were more than powerful enough for either of the Lanes services. (D. R. Harvey Collection)

Car 53

Standing alongside St Michael's church in St Michael's Street is one of the original combination single-deck cars of 1904. It is 17 November 1929 and this is the last tram to run to Oldbury along Moor Street and Bromford Lane from West Bromwich. On the following morning the trams were replaced by West Bromwich Corporation single-deck buses on a new circular service from West Bromwich via Bromford Lane to Oldbury, then to Spon Croft and going back to Dartmouth Square via Spon Lane; the route also operated in the opposite direction. This was the terminus of the Bromford Lane route and was linked to the West Bromwich High Street tram tracks in the background by a single service curve. (D. R. Harvey Collection)

Smethwick, Oldbury and Dudley Route

Birmingham to Cape Hill

Car 209

On Saturday 30 September 1939, just three weeks into the Second World War, a line of four trams stood at the impressive loading shelters on Edmund Street at the terminus of the Dudley Road tram services. This was the last day of tramcar operation on these routes. The leading tram is working on the 85 service to Spon Lane. It is an open-balconied ex-Radial truck car, 209, built by UEC in 1907, which would be withdrawn at the end of this day and placed in store at Rosebery Street Depot as a reserve car for the rest of the war. The building on the left is the Gas Hall, which is protected from bomb blast by sandbags. Opposite is a signpost pointing to the nearest ARP air-raid shelter. (D. R. Harvey Collection)

Car 112 *(Top)*

The terminus for the Dudley Road routes and those inherited from Birmingham & Midland Tramways which ran outside the city boundary to Smethwick, Oldbury, Tividale and Dudley was in Edmund Street, where trams stood alongside the Corporation Water Department offices, which formed part of the Council House extension opened in 1885. On Tuesday 30 August 1938, UEC-built tramcar 112 of 1906 is being chased by an intended passenger as it moves off on the 85 route to Spon Lane, West Smethwick. Within a year this tram had been broken up at West Smethwick depot by Cashmores of Great Bridge. (W. A. Camwell)

Car 124 *(Opposite below)*

From the bottom of Cape Hill at the city boundary to Dudley was 6.17 route miles. The conductor of Car 124 has turned the trolley pole prior to the tram being driven over the crossover and on to the left-hand track before returning to Birmingham on the 55 route. This was the original terminus, at Grove Lane city boundary, of the Corporation tram route first opened to traffic on 1 July 1906, although Corporation trams ran as far as Windmill Lane at the top of the distant Cape Hill as well as exclusively on the branch to Bearwood. Car 124 was an open-balcony radial truck built by UEC in late 1906, but was fitted with a Brush-built Peckham P35 truck and BTH GE 249A 37 hp motors in the mid-1920s. It was one of 150 top-covered trams with a seating capacity of fifty-two. On the right is the Cape of Good Hope Public House, dating from December 1925, located on the site of an old ale house and directly opposite the Mitchell's & Butler's Brewery. (W. A. Camwell)

B&M 20 *(Above)*

Climbing up Cape Hill from the Cape Hill brewery towards Windmill Lane is Birmingham & Midland Tramways 'Aston' type Car 20. This was one of many Aston-type double-deckers built by the Brush Company in 1904 for all the affiliated Birmingham and Black Country tramway companies. This forty-eight-seater was mounted on a Brush-built Lycett & Conaty 8-foot 6-inch radial truck. When new, it was equipped with Raworth Regenerative braking but this was removed after 1908, when Birmingham Corporation objected to the use of the system as it fed power back into the system and caused surges in the power supply. They were fitted with top covers during the period between 1908 and 1923, re-motored, re-trucked and fitted with a semi-enclosed platform screen. Car 20, appropriately carrying a Mitchells & Butler advertisement below the open balcony, is passing the school on the corner of Durban Road. (D. R. Harvey Collection)

Car 195 *(Top)*

Approaching Salisbury Road with the towered Barclays Bank on the corner, Car 195 climbs up Cape Hill towards Windmill Lane when working on the 86 route to Oldbury. The shops, including Woolworth's Bazaar on the left, have all got their blinds pulled down on this warm summer's day in the early 1930s. The tram had been 'native' to Rosebery Street depot prior to the takeover of the B&M services on 1 April 1928 and was not one of the thirty-six cars drafted into West Smethwick in the autumn of that year when the trams hired from B&M were returned. (Commercial Postcard)

Car 136 *(Opposite below)*
UEC former radial truck tramcar 136 is going straight across the Windmill Lane junction at Cape Hill as it travels on its way to Oldbury and Dudley on the 87 route in about 1937. It will pass the policeman on point duty, who is wearing a cap that is of a different design to those worn by police in Birmingham. Cape Hill was a busy suburban shopping centre, with many of the large retailers having thriving premises around the junction. On the corner of Windmill Lane is a George Mason grocery shop, replacing the earlier Universal Tea Company, while next door, originating from the same town, is the West Bromwich Building Society. Opposite, and slightly obscured by the ornate lamp standard in the foreground, is the Seven Stars Hotel. On the right of the junction, on the corner of Shireland Road, is Marsh & Baxter's, the well-known Birmingham-based pork butchers. The tracks in the right foreground take the 29 tram service to Bearwood. (Commercial Postcard)

B&M 22 *(Above)*
Until 1906 there was a large eighteenth-century house partially hidden from the junction of Waterloo Road on the left and Cape Hill by a number of large elm trees; thus the house was appropriately named The Elms. The tram route to Windmill Lane was opened on 21 November 1904, while the tracks on the left to Bearwood, along the residential Waterloo Road, opened just three days later. B&M 22, a Brush-built Aston-type open-top tramcar, was delivered at the same time as the route opening in 1904 and shows 'WINDMILL LANE' on the destination box. The second open-topper negotiating the cross-over is CBT Car 214, which was on loan in the spring of 1905 to B&M, who were short of new tramcars. Car 214 would eventually become BCT's 483, having been completely rebuilt with a top-cover and vestibule platform, lasting until withdrawal in March 1939, thus almost surviving throughout the life of the electric tram services on Dudley Road. (D. R. Harvey Collection)

CAPE HILL, SMETHWICK.

B&M 4 *(Top)*

The area around Cape Hill at the Windmill Lane junction was developed as a shopping centre at the turn of the twentieth century. The large gabled premises on the right which continued into Windmill Lane were occupied by the Universal Tea Company, purveyors of groceries and provisions. The large house behind the trees between Waterloo Road and the high street was called The Elms and was demolished in about 1906 to make way for the Lloyds Bank building that still occupies the site. On the left is Waterloo Road, which had no tram tracks, thus dating the photograph to before 24 November 1904, when the Birmingham & Midland Tramways Company opened their service to Bearwood. The two tramcars are standing at the B&M's short-working terminus at Windmill Lane. The tram to the left is B&M Car 4, a Brush-built car of October 1904, running on Brush AA-type rigid trucks. It has been fitted with a Dick, Kerr 'Bellamy'-style short, uncanopied top-cover

developed by the General Manager of Liverpool Corporation. The open-top car to the right it is City of Birmingham Tramways Company tramcar 211 or 213. It was delivered in November 1904 and was presumably on loan to the Birmingham & Midland when new, within weeks of the opening of the electric tram services to Smethwick. The leaves on the trees would mean that it wasn't November. However, on another copy the leaves are not there – they were painted on the postcard! (Commercial Postcard)

Car 72 *(Opposite below)*

The imposing Lloyds Bank at the apex of Bearwood Hill and Waterloo Road was built in 1907 on the site of the large Georgian house known as The Elms. In about 1930, BCT Car 72, a UEC-bodied forty-eight-seat tram originally mounted on M&G Radial trucks, stands at the Windmill Road junction. It has arrived on an 80 route short working from St Paul's Road, Smethwick, and stands just beyond the former entrance to the B&M steam tram depot. By this time Car 72 had been mounted on Brush-built Peckham P35 trucks in about 1926. Behind the tramcar is Bearwood Hill with a row of three-storey Victorian shops with gabled attics. (Commercial Postcard)

B&M 13 *(Above)*

Loading up with passengers at Cape Hill in about 1906 is B&M open-top Car 13. These basic-looking tramcars were built in 1904 by the Loughborough-based tram builder Brush, and this was the first of the six trams which never received top-covers. When new, these trams were used on the Spon Lane service from West Bromwich. Car 13 is standing in front of the row of shops between Windmill Lane and the entrance to the former B&M coke yard, constructed in about 1901. The tram is about to leave for Birmingham. (D. R. Harvey Collection)

B&M 59 *(Opposite above)*

On an Edwardian summer's day in about 1906, B&M single-deck Car 59, a Kyotts Lake Road Works-built closed-combination tram with a monitor-style roof and an 8-foot 6-inch Lycett & Conaty Radial truck, is working on the wrong track towards Smethwick. In the distance is a B&M Aston-type double-decker, which could be Car 20, which is on its way towards Oldbury by way of the nearby Victoria Park and Rolf Street Station. This is because of road works blocking the track between Waterloo Road and the distant Claremont Road. On the right is the Gospel Hall with its tall gabled roof, which is adjacent to the entrance to the Windmill Lane steam tram coking yard. (J. H. Taylforth)

Car 215 *(Opposite below)*

In High Street, on the west side of the Cape Hill junction with Windmill Lane, is UEC-bodied ex-M&G Radial Car 215. The tram is waiting to return from this important shopping centre to the city on service 30. Just visible on the other side of the junction are trams coming up the steep hill from Grove Lane. 215 had been transferred from Coventry Road depot to Rosebery Street depot, where it remained until it was withdrawn in April 1939. (W. A. Camwell)

B&M Steam Tram *(Above)*

Looking towards Cape Hill from the Smethwick end of the high street in about 1902 is a B&M Kitson steam tram pulling a double-deck trailer. Standing at the top of Bearwood Hill, the tram is travelling on the Smethwick-bound track at Windmill Lane. On the left is the impressive Market Place building, which later became the Co-Operative Society. The tall trees behind the tram are elms, which gave their name to the large eighteenth-century house which was demolished in 1906. (Commercial Postcard)

Smethwick

Car 88

The 1936-registered Armstrong-Siddeley Twelve-Plus, parked opposite Smethwick Council House, was priced when new at £320. On the far side of High Street are the gates of the 35-acre Victoria Park, opened in 1888. Its cottage-style gatehouse reflects the architectural style of the arts and crafts movement that was frequently used in parks towards the end of the nineteenth century. It is Wednesday 12 April 1939 and UEC-bodied former Radial tramcar 88, one of forty-five cars of the 71 Class assigned to West Smethwick depot, has come down the hill from Cape Hill junction on the 87 service to Dudley. (H. B. Priestley)

B&M 5

Near to Smethwick Council House, B&M tramcar 5, one of the original open-top Brush-built company trams from the 1-12 series of 1904, about four years after it was constructed, passes the original Red Cow public house in High Street. The tramcar is heading towards West Smethwick and Oldbury. The ivy-covered house on the left was at the junction with Watery Lane, but was soon demolished in order to widen the main road. (Commercial Postcard)

B&M 48 (Left)

At the Blue Gates Public House, B&M Car 48, one of the Birmingham & Midland Aston-type top-covered cars of 1904, travels along High Street on its way to Oldbury in about 1913. It had been fitted with a flat roofed top-cover built at Tividale Works in about 1908. The tram has just passed Smethwick Reading Library and the Blue Gates Hotel, whose sign can be seen near the large lantern-shaped street light on the corner of Stony Lane. There has recently been a heavy rainstorm that has left the pavements very wet, but even more noticeably the mud on the road is more reminiscent of Dodge City rather than Smethwick! (Commercial Postcard)

Car 159 *(Opposite below)*
Car 159 has arrived from Birmingham on the 86 route to Oldbury in September 1939 and is standing opposite the George Inn on the north side of High Street, at the corner of Brasshouse Lane. Two weeks into the Second World War and white, road markings on kerbs and street furniture have been painted in order to help pedestrians and traffic during hours of darkness. The tram has also had its fender painted white, but has not been fitted with a headlight mask. Two weeks later, the Dudley routes were abandoned and the trams temporarily placed in store in case the routes might be reinstated under wartime measures. Car 159, along with the other forty-nine of the class that ended up at West Smethwick, was broken up in early 1940 by Cashmores of Great Bridge. (Newman College)

B&M 46 *(Above)*
The high street in West Smethwick was a bustling shopping centre throughout the years of tramcar operation. Birmingham & Midland Tramways Car 46, one of the Brush-built Aston-type four-wheelers, in its final mid-1920s condition, is fitted with an enclosed top deck from the late Edwardian era and a front vestibule screen put in place just after the First World War to partially protect the driver. Here, it heads away from the St Paul's Road junction as it proceeds through the shopping centre towards Cape Hill and Birmingham. (D. R. Harvey Collection)

Car 197 *(Top)*

High Street, Smethwick, was a bustling shopping centre that gradually declined in importance after the Second World War. 1906-built UEC-bodied four-wheel Car 197 has worked into Smethwick on the 80 service on 2 July 1938, and is at the western end of the high street at its junction with St Paul's Road, where the 80 service terminated. Travelling from the Birmingham direction is another of the Corporation's 71 Class. It is working on the 85 route to Spon Lane. This is Car 192, which is being passed on the nearside by an Austin Big Seven saloon. Tram 197 outlived 192 by just two months when it was withdrawn in May 1939 and both were broken up at West Smethwick depot by Cashmores about two months after the closure of the Track tram services on 30 September 1939. (H. B. Priestley)

B&M 7 *(Opposite below)*

It is probable that this is 24 November 1904, which was the opening day of Birmingham & Midland electric tram operations between Lionel Street in Birmingham and Dudley. This is almost certainly why the driver and conductor, as well as the two smocked young girls, are posing at the St Paul's Road terminus in Smethwick, as it was quite common that such important occasions were recorded for posterity. Car 7 was one of twelve of the original 1–18 batch of tramcars fitted with Bellamy-type top-covers originally designed by the Liverpool General Manager, C. R. Bellamy, and is mounted on a rigid Brush AA-type truck. (Whitcombe Collection)

Car 98 *(Above)*

Travelling towards St Paul's Road, having left the terminus of the 85 route at Spon Lane, just over ½ mile away, is UEC-bodied former M&G Radial truck tramcar 98. The tram is going towards Smethwick on the interlaced track on Oldbury Road. It is Saturday 30 September 1939 and this would be the final day of tramcar operation on the Track, the nickname given to the services formerly operated by the Birmingham & Midland Tramways Company. On the following day, this part of the route would almost become the complete domain of a new fleet of Midland Red SOS FEDDs with forward-entrance Brush bodywork operated from the still fairly new Oldbury garage. Behind the tram and beyond the petrol station, a large Vauxhall 25 GY six-cylinder saloon is turning into Roebuck Lane, where it will use the magnificent Thomas Telford-designed Galton Bridge of 1828 with its huge 150-foot span to cross the Birmingham Level of the Birmingham Canal Navigation, some 71 feet below. (L. W. Perkins)

Car 189 *(Top)*

Car 189 is working on the 87 service and is travelling towards Dudley in the last few days of tramcar operation in late September 1939. It is about to pass the garage premises of Roebuck Engineering, on the corner of Roebuck Lane, and head directly on to Galton Bridge. There were only four places on the Birmingham tram system where operation was controlled by signal lights, and three of them were on the Oldbury route. At Oldbury Road, near Smethwick Junction Station, the road narrowed over the former GWR's Stourbridge Extension line from The Hawthorns Halt Station, resulting in the interlacing of the tram tracks over the bridge. A broken white line between the four tramlines was there to remind drivers of the track layout. Car 189 was one of eighteen of the 71 Class cars allocated to Rosebery Street and had been allocated to that depot since it arrived from Highgate Road depot in 1935. (Newman College)

B&M 2 (Opposite below)

Carrying advertisements for a military parade with the Irish Guards at Summerfield Park in the lower saloon, and one in the Bellamy top-covered windows for travelling by tram to Kinver, is B&M Car 2. This was one of the twelve Brush-bodied open-top trams of 1904 to be fitted with one of these open balcony top covers and is equipped with Brush AA 6 foot 6 inch wheelbase rigid trucks. The tram is carrying an advertisement for Dunville's VR, which was a rare, pure, pot still whiskey, distilled at the Royal Irish Distillery in Belfast until 1936. The tram has a destination blind showing 'Spon Lane' but appears to be in Oldbury Road, working on the mainline route from Birmingham. (D. R. Harvey Collection)

Oldbury

Car 102 (Above)

A UEC ex-M&G Radial truck car, 102, stands at the Spon Lane 85 route short working terminus in Oldbury Road, just west of the Spon Croft, on 2 July 1938. The original eighteenth-century building was located on the Smethwick side of the junction and was replaced in 1935 by a larger public house on the left, behind the tram. The old, derelict Spon Lane Tavern is in the distance and was not demolished for a number of years. Until the closure of the single-deck operated B&M tram routes along Spon Lane and Bromford Lane in Oldbury on 17 November 1929, there was a reversing triangle at the Spon Lane junction with Oldbury Road which enabled the trams to reverse back to West Bromwich and also gain access to West Smethwick depot and Tividale Works. (Birmingham Central Reference Library)

Car 84 *(Above)*

At the corner of Hawthorn Street in Oldbury Road, is UEC-built Car 84, constructed in 1906, which had arrived in 1929 at West Smethwick depot and worked from there until withdrawn on 30 September 1939. On Wednesday 12 April 1939, the tram is working on the 86 service to Oldbury, which had been taken over from the B&M on 1 April 1928. On the left is the London Screw Company factory, which made fixings, while opposite on the right is Oldbury Road Board School. Going towards Smethwick is a brand new Fordson E83W 10 cwt van on West Bromwich trade plates and following the tram is a new Morris Eight car. (H. B. Priestley)

B&M 4 *(Opposite below)*
Travelling along Oldbury Road towards Oldbury in the mid-1920s, on one of the single-track sections near to West Smethwick depot, is Birmingham & Midland top-covered tramcar 4. This Brush-bodied tram was equipped with a style of driver's windscreen which was fitted to many of the associated Black Country company trams. These did not fully enclose the platform and left the staircase side open to the elements. To the left, the factory building is part of the Chance Glassworks. Chance Bros was founded in 1824 in Spon Lane, Smethwick. During the nineteenth century it became one of the most important glassworks in Britain. It manufactured the panes for the Crystal Palace of 1851, window glass in different colours and optical glass, including the lenses for lighthouses. Most of the furnaces and cones were demolished in the late 1940s. (D. R. Harvey Collection)

Car 107 *(Above)*
On Friday 23 September 1939, with just over one week left of tramcar operation on the Dudley route, UEC-bodied ex-Radial Car 107 stands outside the gloomy sheds of West Smethwick depot. The Corporation 71 Class trams had been used on the routes taken over from the Birmingham & Midland Company on 1 April 1928. They were very short of trams at this time and although it had ordered fifty bogie cars (to be numbered 762–811), it had to hire all the thirty-eight trams allocated by the company to West Smethwick depot in order to maintain the services. Gradually, during the next few months, the Corporation managed to get enough 71 Class cars together, transferring them from depots, so that the company trams could be returned, mainly for scrap. (J. S. Webb)

Car 108

Looking towards Oldbury, with a new bus stop plate already in position outside the entrance to West Smethwick depot, it is the final day of operation of trams services on The Track, thereby becoming the last group of tram services in the Black Country to remain in operation. These routes had survived as the remnants of a once large narrow-gauge tram system, the rest having finally succumbed to the bus some nine years before. Car 108, a UEC-bodied former M&G Radial truck car, by now thirty-three years old and fitted with Brush Peckham P35 trucks, stands on the depot entrance triangle tracks on its way towards Oldbury and Dudley on service 87. (R. T Coxon)

Car 148 *(Left)*

Beyond the Spon Lane junction was West Smethwick depot, whose curved entrance tracks are in the foreground. The depot had been used by BCT from 1 April 1928, along with the 6.17 route miles from Grove Lane to Dudley. Car 148, on its way from Dudley to Birmingham via Smethwick on an 87 service, has stopped to pick up workmen. It is Thursday 14 April 1938 and UEC-bodied Car 148 would run for another thirteen months before being withdrawn in May 1939. (H. B. Priestley)

Cars 129 and 88

In West Smethwick depot yard on 14 April 1938 are BCT cars 129 and 88. Both of these trams had been allocated to West Smethwick depot in July 1928, 88 coming from Washwood Heath and 129 from Coventry Road. These 71 Class tramcars belonged to a batch of 150 trams bought by Birmingham Corporation Tramways; all entered service between August 1906 and March 1907. The bodies, which were top-covered from new, were fifty-two-seaters and from the mid-1920s both were mounted on Brush-built Peckham P35 trucks, remotored with BTH GE 249A 37 hp motors and fitted with platform vestibules. (H. B. Priestley)

Car 216, 151, Etc

Standing in the yard of West Smethwick depot on 7 April 1939 is Car 162. Parked inside the depot are 216, 151, 74, 112, 186 and 94. West Smethwick depot had a normal capacity of around forty-five trams but after the withdrawal of the trams on the Dudley services, all the Rosebery Street depot trams were taken to West Smethwick to be broken up, giving a total capacity of withdrawn trams of nearly eighty. Parked on the extreme right is the former B&M stores tram, which had been withdrawn in 1927. (L. W. Perkins)

Car 162 *(Above)*
Birmingham Corporation Tramways and Omnibus Department took over the operation of the routes through Smethwick and used the former Birmingham & Midland Tramways depot in West Smethwick. In West Smethwick depot yard on 7 April 1939 is UEC-bodied Car 162, mounted on Brush Peckham P35 trucks. Trams returning to West Smethwick depot usually displayed the destination 'Spon Lane 85', rather than the more usual 'Depot Only'. Despite the tram looking in good condition, this was 162's last 'professional' appearance as it was driven into the depot and withdrawn. This was due to the hiatus the previous week when, after the Hockley depot's routes were withdrawn, the transferring of their bogie trams and the cascading of older trams ensured the withdrawal of the 71 Class cars. After a week of tramcar movements, the first tranche of thirty-three 71 Class tramcar withdrawals took place, with 162 being one of them. The final withdrawals at the end of September 1939 accounted for fifty-six of these trams. (H. B. Priestley)

Car 124 *(Opposite above)*
The main A457 road between Smethwick and Sedgley used to be part of the main road between Birmingham and Wolverhampton before the Birmingham New Road was opened by HRH Prince Edward, Prince of Wales, on 2 November 1927. It passed through the centre of Oldbury via Birmingham Street before arriving at the Market Place. The last day of tramcar operation was 30 September 1939, as normal a busy Saturday shopping day as was possible with the war just over three weeks old. Car 124 passes Church Square when working on the 87 service towards Dudley. It will be using the bus stop, which has yet to be painted with wartime white stripes. The iron railings in front of Christ Church, Oldbury's parish church, dating from 1840, were lost the following year in the wartime scrap metal drive. (R. T. Coxon)

B&M 19 *(Right)*

Towards the Market Place end of Birmingham Street, the road through the middle of Oldbury was so narrow that the tram tracks were laid so that trams travelling could not pass each other. In later years, this section of the line was controlled by signal light. Travelling into Oldbury from Birmingham is B&M open-top Car 19. This tram was the first of the company's Brush-built open-top four-wheelers, known as Aston types. They were delivered in November 1904 and fitted with 8-foot 6-inch wheelbase Lycett & Conaty Radial axle trucks. These were rebuilt after about a decade due to their poor riding qualities and in later life were quite highly regarded. Behind the tram is the Junction public house on the corner of the distant Unity Place and Birmingham Street. (Commercial Postcard)

Car 154 *(Above)*

In Birmingham Street, Oldbury, working from the Municipal Buildings in the Market Place on the 87 route on 23 August 1939, is tramcar 154. The tram has just crossed over the pinch points to enter the short section of interlaced track that were controlled by traffic lights. Towards the Market Place end of Birmingham Street, the road became much narrower and the tram tracks had to be laid very close together. The section of the route from Unity Place to the Market Place, although double-track, was operated as a single-line section because trams were unable to pass. This section was controlled by coloured signal lights which were operated by actuators on the overhead. Car 154 is about halfway along this section of Birmingham Street. (W. A. Camwell)

Car 186 *(Opposite above)*

Crossing the open space of the Market Place in Oldbury is BCT four-wheel tramcar 186. This 71 Class tram of 1907 is arriving at its Oldbury terminus alongside the Municipal Buildings in Freeth Street, just beyond the 1935 Standard Sixteen. Parked in the bus station in front of the Municipal Buildings is a Midland Red SOS FEDD-type double-decker in its smartly lined-out livery which is about to depart for Halesowen. To the left of the view is Church Street, which leads to Bromford Lane. This had been served until 1929 by a single-deck tram route operated by the Birmingham & Midland Company, the curve of the setts still marking the line of this abandoned route. (W. A. Camwell)

Car 84

Leaving Oldbury Market Place as it crosses from Freeth Street into Birmingham Street is UEC Car 84. It is working on the 87 service from Dudley to Birmingham during what appears to be the celebrations for the Coronation of King George VI in May 1937, except for one thing and that is the parked Standard Twelve parked at the entrance to Birmingham Street. This has the Birmingham registration letters EOB, which were not issued until March 1938! So why all the bunting and Union flags? (W. A. Camwell)

Tividale

Car 80 *(Above)*

Former Radial Car 80 is about to leave the passing loop in Dudley Road East, near Brades Village. It is working from Oldbury on the 87 route towards Oldbury in the summer of 1939. Behind the tram, the surrounding derelict land west of Oldbury had been derelict for many years and bore testimony to the decline in the primary and heavy industry in the Black Country during the Depression years of the late 1920s and the early 1930s, caused by the exhaustion of the locally extracted raw materials, with many old coal tips lining the road. (K. Lane)

Car 92 *(Opposite above)*

Car 92, a former M&G Radial truck tram with an open-balcony UEC body, is about to enter a passing loop near Brades Locks on Dudley Road East at Brades Village. Car 92, seen on 23 September 1939, is working on the 87 service towards Oldbury and, like the street furniture, has had its fender painted white as part of the wartime measures to make it more visible in the blackout. This tramcar had been at Coventry Road depot throughout the 1920s but due to the closure of the routes operated by Hockley depot, the cascading of trams around the system resulted in the 71 Class tramcars being replaced on the Stechford services by the low-height 301 Class trams. Thus Car 92 was moved to West Smethwick depot on or just after 8 April 1939, where it remained in service until the route closed on the last day of September; it would be dismantled by Cashmores in April 1940. (J. S. Webb)

Car 107

Working on the 87 route to Dudley on 12 April 1939 is 1906-vintage Car 107. These trams were built with top-covers, but during the 1920s were rebuilt with Brush-built Peckham P35 trucks, increased horse power motors and enclosed platforms. It is seen at the entrance tracks to the former Birmingham & Midland Tividale tram depot and works. Tividale Works opened on 1 January 1907 and finally closed down in March 1930, but the track and the overhead remained in situ for feeder purposes from the sub-station in the depot yard until the end of tramcar operation on the route. (H. B. Priestley)

B&M 1-12 Car

The tram, parked in Tividale depot yard in 1921, is one of the B&M 1-12 open-top tramcars built by Brush in 1904 and fitted with the quite short Brush AA 6 foot 6 inch-long trucks, which would have given a tail-wagging ride on anything other than good quality tracks. The tram was at one time fitted with a short Bellamy top-cover, though this was removed after a few years. The change in the style of railings along the upper saloon from those on the balconies is evidence of this conversion back to open top. The tram is fitted with the very basic driver's window devised by the B&M and latterly used throughout the Black Country tram system which left the sides of the platforms open to the elements. (W. Gratwicke)

B&M Car 20

Climbing Tividale Road, within a couple of years of the end of company operations, is company Car 20. It has just passed the Tividale tram works, which stood in the shadow of the distant St Michael's church. The tram is approaching Burnt Tree, where it will meet the tram route from West Bromwich before running over the former South Staffordshire Tramways tracks for the final run into Dudley. This Brush-built Aston-type tram, built in 1904, was originally an open-topper, but was extensively rebuilt with a Tividale-built top-cover, roller blind destination boxes over the platform and 35 hp motors. This was one of the thirty-eight company cars hired to BCT after the route was taken over from April until August 1928. On 1 April 1928, the Birmingham & Midland operation of the Birmingham–Oldbury–Dudley route was taken over by Birmingham Corporation. (R. Bennett)

Midland Metro

24

Having arrived at the Hawthorns Midland Metro stop, car 24, one of the CAF Urbos 3 trams has loaded up with passengers. It is about to head towards West Bromwich on 11 January 2015. The heritage of this section of line is easily apparent as it was originally opened by the Great Western Railway as The Hawthorns Halt in 1931 to serve the West Bromwich Albion football ground on match days. It lasted in this form until 1968 whereupon it closed, not reopening until 1995 as part of the Jewellery Line. This Network Rail line is on the left and curves away to the left towards the next station at Galton Bridge. The Metro line follows the line of the old GWR main line to Wolverhampton. (D. R. Harvey)

26
Standing at the Hawthorns on 11 January 2015 is car 26 which was in its first few days of
service. It is travelling towards Birmingham and clearly shows the five section composition
of these second generation Midland Metro trams. The covered over-bridge connects the
Metro and Network Rail Stations, the latter being on the extreme right. (D. R. Harvey)

15
At West Bromwich Central Metro Station on 18 January 2006 is tram 15, the penultimate
Ansaldobreda T69 articulated two-section trams of 1999. The tram is about to leave to
go on to the next station at Lodge Road. (D. R. Harvey)

22
Arriving at West Bromwich Central on 2 January 2015 is tram 22. This CAF Urbos 3 has seating for just fifty-four passengers on somewhat uncomfortable seats. Tram 22 is travelling towards Birmingham and stands sat the Metro stop with West Bromwich Bus Station hidden by the tram. (D. R. Harvey)

23
The use of existing infrastructure dating back to the days of the Great Western Railway was in principle a good one as tram 23 arrives at Lodge Road tram stop from Wednesbury on 11 January 2015, but the logistics of getting down to the platform is limited by using either a tiny lift or the multi-level staircase around the lift tower. (D. R. Harvey)

08

Leaving the Dudley Street, Gun's Village metro stop on 11 January 2015 is car 08, named *Joseph Chamberlain*. This is the nearest tram stop to Carter's Green. This Ansaldobreda tram is travelling to Black Lake and is about to pass beneath the Dudley Street Bridge which takes the 74 bus route from Birmingham and West Bromwich to Dudley. (D. R. Harvey)

05

Standing at Wednesbury Station on 29 January 1999 is Ansaldobreda T69 car 05. The brand new tram is on a driver training duty some four months before the public services commenced. It is alongside new trams in the yard of the Wednesbury depot. (D. R. Harvey)

Birmingham Corporation Tramcar Fleet Operating on the West Bromwich Routes 1924–39

21–70

Built 1905–6

221–300

Built 1907–8

UEC open-top, three-bay bodies, open platforms. Seating capacity twenty-six/twenty-two. Mounted on Brill 21E 6-foot trucks. Dick, Kerr DK25 25 hp motors. Top-covers fitted to all 1911–25, except 266, which was used as the Illuminated Car 1909–29. All except twenty-eight cars vestibuled 1925–8. Cars 41–70/221–222/234/237–239/243–244/247–252/254–256/259–265 fitted with Maley track brake 1909–10. Most Brill-Maleys fitted with Dick, Kerr DK13A 40 hp motors 1919–22. Various cars fitted with Fischer bow-collectors from 1924. Car 28 cut down to single-deck for 1916 trailer experiments. Withdrawals July 1930 – May 1937; last withdrawals of Lodge Road Brill-Maleys with bow-collectors May 1947.

71–220

Built 1906-7

UEC top-covered, four-bay bodies with open balconies and platforms. Seating capacity twenty-eight/twenty-four. Mounted on Mountain & Gibson 8-foot 6-inch radial trucks. All re-trucked 1925–28, Dick, Kerr 6A 55 hp motors. Cars 82/101/146/152/165/213 with UEC Preston trucks. Cars 89/115/125/157–158/161/168/175/208 with Brush trucks. All remaining 135 cars fitted with Brush Peckham P35 pendulum trucks. All vestibuled 1925–50. From 1926, 102 cars fitted with BTH GE249A 35 hp motors. Twenty-one cars fitted with DK13A 40 hp motors 1934–7. Withdrawals January 1937 – September 1939. Cars 73/87/89/97/99/104/109/111/113/116/125/137/142/144/160/170/172/176-7/183/207/210 retained for emergency use throughout Second World War.

512–586

Built 1913–4

UEC four-bay bodies with open balconies. Seating capacity thirty-four/twenty-eight. Mounted on M&G Burnley bogies. Dick, Kerr DK19A 40 hp motors. Balconies enclosed

1926–30. Cars 512–562/5–6 fitted with BTH GE249A 37 hp motors 1918–22. Car 563 fitted with DK30B 40 hp motors 1920. Cars 564/67–86 fitted with Dick, Kerr DK13A 40 hp motors 1920–3. Cars 537–562/5–6 fitted with Dick, Kerr DK30/1L 63 hp motors 1925–7. Cars 512–536 fitted with GEC WT 32R 70 hp motors 1927–8. EMB Burnley bogies and Dick, Kerr DK30B 40 hp motors fitted to cars 551/69–73/6–81/3–6 1943–51. Cars 564/67–8/74–5/82 destroyed in air raids 1941. Cars 525/538 withdrawn in Second World War; rest of class withdrawn 1950–3.

587–636
Built 1920–1
Brush four-bay bodies with open balconies. Seating capacity thirty-four/twenty-eight. Mounted on Brush Burnley bogies. BTH GE 249A 37 hp motors. Balconies enclosed 1927–31. Car 630 equipped with EMB Maley air-brakes 1923. Withdrawn 1949–53.

Birmingham City Transport
Route Numbers

23

Colmore Row to The Hawthorns, Handsworth, 1 July 1911. Abandoned 1 April 1939. Replaced by 72 bus service.

28

Colmore Row to New Inns, Crocketts Lane, Handsworth, 1 July 1911. Short working of 23 route. Abandoned 1 April 1959. Replaced by 71 bus service.

30

Edmund Street to Windmill Lane, Cape Hill, Smethwick. Joint service with Birmingham & Midland 24 November 1904 as short working of 29 route but operated entirely by BCT. Abandoned 30 September 1939. Replaced by B81 bus service.

73

Livery Street to Carters Green, West Bromwich, 1 April 1924. Short working of 74 and 75 services. Abandoned 1 April 1939. Replaced by 73 bus service.

74

Livery Street to Dudley (Tipton Road) via West Bromwich. Ex-South Staffordshire (Lessee) service 20 December 1902 – 31 March 1924. Taken over by BCT 1 April 1924. Abandoned 1 April 1939. Replaced by 74 bus service.

75

Livery Street to Wednesbury (White Horse). Part of South Staffordshire (Lessee) service 20 December 1902 – 31 March 1924. Taken over by BCT 1 April 1924. Abandoned 1 April 1939. Replaced by 75 bus route.

76

Colmore Row to Great Bridge 1925. Short working of 74 service. Abandoned 1 April 1939. Replaced by 76 bus service.

77

Colmore Row to Spon Lane/High Street, West Bromwich, 1925. Short working of 75, 74, 75 and 76 services. Abandoned 1 April 1939. Replaced by 77 bus service.

80

Edmund Street to St Paul's Road, Smethwick. Ex-Birmingham & Midland. Short working of 87 service. Taken over by BCT 1 April 1928. Abandoned 30 September 1939. Replaced by B84 bus service.

85

Edmund Street to Spon Lane, West Bromwich, via Smethwick. Ex-Birmingham & Midland, 24 November 1904. Short working of 87 service. Taken over by BCT 1 April 1928. Abandoned 30 September 1939. Replaced by B85 bus service.

86

Edmund Street to Oldbury via Smethwick. Ex-Birmingham & Midland, 24 November 1904. Short working of 87 service. Taken over by BCT 1 April 1928. Abandoned 30 September 1939. Replaced by B86 service.

87

Edmund Street to Dudley (Tipton Road) via Smethwick and Oldbury. Ex-Birmingham & Midland, 24 November 1904. Taken over by BCT 1 April 1928. Abandoned 30 September 1939. Replaced by B87 bus service.

88

Windmill Lane to Spon Lane, West Bromwich, via Smethwick. Ex-Birmingham & Midland, 24 November 1904. Taken over by BCT 1 April 1928. Short working of 87 service. Abandoned 30 September 1939. Replaced by B88 bus route.

Company Trams Used on the West Bromwich Area Routes

Birmingham & Midland Tramways Ltd

1–12
Bellamy roof. Brush twenty-two/twenty-four. Brush AA truck. Brush 1002B two x 33 hp. Built 1904.

13–18
Open top Brush twenty-two/twenty-four. Brush AA truck. Brush 1002B two x 33 hp. Built 1904.

19–24
Open top Brush twenty-two/twenty-six. Brush Conaty truck. Brush 1002B two x 33 hp. Built 1904.

25–50
Open top Brush twenty-two/twenty-six. Brush Conaty truck. Brush 1002B two x 33 hp. Built 1904.

53–60
Single-deck combination. CBT thirty-four seats. Brush Conaty truck. Brush 1002B two x 33 hp. Built 1904.

51–52, 1–2 (ii)
Single-deck two compartments. BMTJC thirty-two seats. Tividale Flexible axle. BTH GE58 two x 37.5 hp. Built 1915.

South Staffordshire Tramways (Lessee) Co. Ltd

1–4
Open top, un-canopied ER & TCW. Twenty-two/twenty-three. Brill 21E trucks. BTH GE800 two x 25 hp, built 1901.